New Life Clarity Publishing

205 West 300 South, Brigham City, Utah 84302

Http://newlifeclarity.com/

Printed in the United States of America

ISBN/SKU: 9780578554709
ISBN Complete: 978-0-578-55470-9

THE INFLUENCE
EFFECT

Created by Eric J. Zuley

In Loving Memory of
Berny Dohrmann

"I just wanted to say a few words about Berny Dohrmann. He was like an industry father to me. I didn't even know him well enough for him to make me feel that way. He was one of those business mentors whose accolades speak for themselves. He edified me in a video, allowing me to resource that video. His edification opened many doors for me with the people that he  knew. The words he spoke about me really were touching, and he did it twice. In doing so, he left a legacy for eZWay. He believed in the positive change that we were promoting. He believed in us. From the bottom of my heart, everything that we are today is thanks to you Berny for helping to provide that stepping stone to that next level of success."

~Eric J. Zuley~

Berny Dohrmann was a fifth generation San Franciscan; and first boy of nine children. Berny's father Alan G. Dohrmann was a pioneer with Dr. Edward Demising in Corporate Total Quality Management, and advanced system modeling for Fortune Institutions worldwide. During

Berny's college years he worked as an apprentice while receiving his post graduate degrees in Economics. Having studied economics with George Witter, Berny apprenticed with Arthur Lachman of Monetary Resources. Steeped with his economic backgrounds, Berny founded Invest America; a full service investment banking firm in the 1960s. In the 1980's Berny took over running his father's global corporate training firm following his father's graduation, and transformed the firm to CEO Space International.

Berny served on the board of the Orlando International Film Festival (OIFF) as a contribution to the arts, and is a principal shareholder and adviser to unicorn founders in breakthrough technologies such as Agriculture, Hydrogen production, Social Hedge Fund development with game changing 5G and AI, Nano technology transforming coal molecular structures into clean burning energy, and many more.

Dedication

---•◦◦•---

To Dad, Dante, and my eZWay Family.

Dad, YOU are my original investor and motivation.

Dante, YOU are my other half. YOU keep me healthy and moving forward.

eZWayFam, YOU are the driving force of the whole eZWay Empire and community.

Table of Contents

Chapter 1

Trendsetter

Before his success, he was just Eric, but even then he was a rare gem. His genius led him to video gaming at an early age. He credits these games for giving him his competitive edge, as well as teaching him how to solve problems. He competed with gamers twice his age, and quickly became known for his gaming skills. He played titles like *Mike Tyson's Punch-Out* and *Mortal Kombat.* Eric excelled when it came to strategy

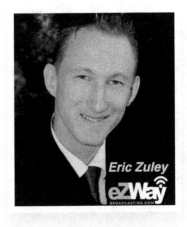

Eric Zuley

games like *Warcraft* and *StarCraft.* They were uniquely challenging as he built cities and conquered kingdoms. He has always stated that gaming was his gateway to business education.

A top sales leader at MBNA America, he has a wide variety of interests, including music, dancing, and sales. He moved toward the business field because his skills and charisma led him to champion others in their pursuit of success. Not only is he an amazing rapper who has written and performed off the cuff, but he also performed with a local dance troupe. Once, when he went to the Garden Grove Hyatt in Orange County, he relished in his moment to dance solo in front of an audience. This performance was watched by a major Hollywood publicist, who happened to be working on a dancing documentary.

She asked him to participate, and Eric was thrilled to be involved. This connection led him to a major Hollywood event, where he met and greeted several Hollywood celebrities, business owners, CEO's and successful entrepreneurs. He attended many other events, where he studied behaviors and learned the proper dos and don'ts of Hollywood.

As he watched and learned, he took on challenges to speak, inspire, and engage with his audiences. As he spoke, he realized he had a gift for communication that could be used to make a real difference.

Star struck and dreaming of financial gains, he was determined to make a name for himself and become the biggest influencer. However, after his father's diagnosis of Stage 4 lymphoma, followed by a near-death experience that severed an artery in his own arm, Eric quickly learned there was more to life than monetary success. He made it his new mission to be of service to others.

Connecting with various actors, celebs, and producers, he trained in radio for six months. This motivated him to create his own radio program. In doing so, he launched an interview show spotlighting top-of-the-line guests with a giant reach. It wasn't long before Eric found himself leading a following of over 8,000 subscribers on his personal YouTube channel.

With over 100,000 Twitter followers, subscribers on YouTube, and his radio show following, Eric learned how to create a multi-platform to propel and promote both corporate and small business owners. He could see successful growth as something within their reach, and he helped them gain momentum. His YouTube Channel, What U Need TV, propelled him to a higher success as he documented all the events and gained a significant following. He learned how to turn his channel into sponsorship opportunities, monetarily as well as with products and leveraged his viewers and subscribers to open more doorways to success.

In his interviews, he showcases others in an effort to spread their inspirational stories. He created a nonprofit organization, the eZWay Cares Foundation. This nonprofit assists international charities, and also serves as another platform for his clients to gain an audience. He has gifted millions of dollars in charity to promote nonprofit messages.

A multimedia mogul, he offers many streaming services that include Roku, and Amazon. His partners include Voice America, Women on TV, Fan TV, as well as various magazines like *Hollywood Weekly* and *Influential People*. He is always using his creative abilities and knowledge to find new platforms that will help his clients reach millions of potential followers all over the world. With his own magazine, a radio show with over 650,000 listeners, and a production of over 275 live events, the millions of dollars he raised for nonprofits has proven to be a blessing for so many.

Eric doesn't just envision the change he wants to heal the world - he wants to inspire others to realize their abilities to make a difference. He encourages growth in each of his clients, and emphasizes sharing positive messages.

Because he understands each client is unique and has different gifts and abilities, he can direct business owners to achieve a higher level of visibility and influence. Eric is a very spiritual person, and is always working in order to serve God's children.

He was dubbed by *Hollywood Weekly* as the "Digital Trailblazer," and was listed as the 7th largest social media influencer. He received the Robert Novak Award from the United States Congress and has graced several visible and prestigious magazine covers, including *The Hollywood Weekly, Soul Central Magazine, Fortune Gazette, The Bizness Magazine, Avant Garde with Shelly Hunt, Business Innova-*

tors Magazine, Influential People Magazine, Small Business Trendset-ters, Worldwide Business Trendsetters, ASK, Digital Journal, The Daily Herald, The Chronicle Journal, and Buzzfeed. Appearances on Fox, E!, EXTRA, TMZ, ABC 7, CBS, ABC, and Telemundo, have also helped to spread his message to thousands.

Eric does it the eZWay and encourages us to do the same. He helps his clients realize their potential in unexpected ways, guiding them to reach new levels of success they would not have found elsewhere.

Chapter 2

———◀◼▶———

The eZWay Effect

by Eric Zuley

1. How can you get more followers?

    a. First, read your audience. Figure out who is sitting in front of you. Are they baby boomers? Do they understand tech? Do you need to show them how to turn on their phones?

    b. Once you've identified your audience, ask them questions to understand what digital means to them. Who has Instagram? Facebook? Do they know how to stream? Ask questions to determine their knowledge of the digital world. Check to see who's raising their hand. That will help to figure out who's following what you're saying.

    c. Next, are they streaming? If they don't know how, this is a great opportunity to teach them. If they have never streamed, this will offer rapid results for follower increase. They'll be absorbing the information you're sharing, and they'll want to join you, in order to gain even more insight.

- Content, content, and more content. If you're talking about speaking and gaining followers, then your content needs to be about speaking and gaining followers! Give incentives. Make it worthwhile for your audience. The more you make it about the audience, the more the audience will engage. When the audience is engaged in the experience, they are more likely to follow you on social media to see what else is happening. Throw the bait out there, make sure you are consistent and are always sharing something new. Get your audience's name, phone number, and email, if possible. Make new contacts. Keep in touch.

- Make these new followers want to go LIVE with you. If you can get 10 people to go LIVE with you, and each person has one thousand followers, this gives you access to about 10,000 people.

- DON'T half-ass your branding. Stop cutting corners, and stay away from Wix or free sites. The low cost will give you low profits. Spend money on an HTML that gives you credibility. Looking the part is more than half the battle.

- Testimonials, case studies, Google searches, and social media followers all contribute to help you make sales. Your logos, brand, and the look of everything surrounding your brand, is huge.

- Your sizzle reel and video should have sold you before you ever stepped onstage. This information is what you want to use to convince them to hire you.

- Don't call yourself an expert unless you are an expert. Show proof that you make people money. Who have you made money? How much money have you made them?

I use television to reach my followers. I show up and express myself on camera. I have over 50 million viewers a month. I have several platforms to offer that help to create better branding and building lasting connections.

2. How can you recognize relationship value vs. monetary value?

   a. Recognizing the power in a Win/win to leverage the relationship.
   b. Sponsorships and the ability to play and get bigger rewards from playing.
   c. Knowing and finding out where the relationship lies.
   d. The power is in the relationship and building the influence. Relationships take many years to build the rapport. People work with those they trust.

Faith, Morals, Integrity and Respect

I gained a great deal of integrity from my upbringing. I've taken the principles I learned as a young man and carried them into the business world. They have shaped everything I've built. Trust is an important part of not only doing business, but forming relationships that are built on a long-term foundation.

Building something—like a charity or cause — and putting so much of yourself into it, creates something people want to follow. It helps you form a movement, tribe, and a community.

So, what is your movement? What are you building? How does it give back?

Appreciate people who have good hearts. You'll attract followers who see your heart, and in turn, they'll want to follow your cause and accompany you on your journey.

So ask yourself: what types of people do you know? Do they trust you? Can your audience fill a room? Are you an expert on something?

Remember: you are who you associate with. It's beneficial to surround yourself with like-minded heartpreneurs. If not, you might damage your credibility before you've even introduced yourself.

I have partnered with God. There's a reason gold is eZWay's official color. The pearly gates of Heaven are gold. eZWay is God's, not mine.

Chapter 3

---●●●---

The Wall of Fame

by Pattie Sadler

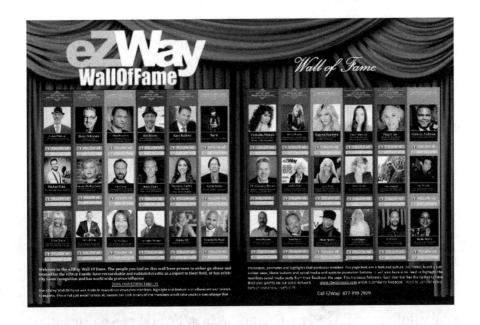

The Wall of Fame, created and designed by Eric J. Zuley has been the moment that all those working with Eric have waited for. The platform creates a space for celebrities and influencers to connect and serve each other with their services. When the eZWay Wall of Fame was launched I was blessed to watch the uprising of something truly special. I watched as amazing handshake deals and connections were made virtually through a portal that included some of the biggest movers and shakers.

Today, Eric Zuley has single handedly structured a space that is better than any other social media experience allowing members to rate each other, collaborate, market their services, and connect on an amazing level. To be a part of this elite group has been one of the highlights of my career.

Not only do members get to come together, but there are plenty of opportunities to get noticed on the wonderful platforms that eZWay has created in the form of virtual events and awards ceremonies. Members get highlighted and receive a large audience to their services. This has been a real eye opening experience for all who are involved.

Joining the eZWay Wall of Fame not only gives you notoriety, but the connections are powerful. It is similar to the Hollywood Walk of Fame only it is digital. Anyone can create an account free and join the Wall of Fame Family. The Wall of Fame gets promoted by our broadcasting network at https://ezwaybroadcasting.com/ which powered our tv network http://ezway.tv, our magazine, https://ezwaymagazine.com.

The eZWay Wall of Fame is a virtual social interactive directory website and mobile app meant to help its members build their following. Certain membership levels allow you to connect and flourish! The eZWay Wall of Fame hosts and annual awards show and honors the members that use their profile to make a difference.

Some of our eZWay Wall of Famers include: Forbes Riley, (Billion Dollar Infomercial Queen), Sharon Lechter, (World re-known author and speaker), Brian J. White, (Actor on OWN Networks Ambitions), Kristanna Loken, (Star of Terminator 3), Alec Stern, (Co-founder of

Constant Contact), and Frank Shankwitz, (Co-founder of Make a Wish Foundation and WISH MAN Movie) Just to name a few.

The eZWay Wall of Fame helps to increase and accelerate influence and brands to go to the next level and get more sales because of the credibility and stature it helps create or add to our members already amazing portfolio.

The wall helps to get its members on other media for more awareness and exposure.

The more that you login, update your profile, share and all around use your account, the higher you go on the wall. This is how you get more traffic to your profile. If you set up your profile to capture and convert, this turns to sales!

To sign up go to https://wall.ezwaybroadcasting.com and join today!

Chapter 4

James Zuley

Parents have a tendency to exaggerate their child's accomplishments, but as Eric's father, I have no reason for exaggeration.

When Eric was very young, I remember pointing out all the homes on a hillside in Laguna Beach. I told him, "Don't just think about buying a home on a hillside, think about owning the development."

I taught him to set goals, stay focused on those goals, and to believe in himself and his own natural abilities. If things aren't working out as planned, no problem. Adjust your strategy and move forward. We all make mistakes, but they are nothing more than stepping stones towards success.

When a plane takes off from New York en route to Los Angeles, it may veer off course, but it adjusts and gets back on track. Over the years, I have tried to inspire Eric to achieve, accomplish, and to help others. I've watched him help so many people reach their goals and change their lives.

I've always believed you need to have determination, drive, and resilience, but those are worth nothing without faith, morals, and ethics.

What I have seen my son accomplish is beyond amazing. I have been in many meetings with Eric and seen his clients' amazed responses when he told them how they could benefit by enhancing their social media presence. He explained how they were not properly utilizing this new technology. The topics he specializes in have always fascinated me.

Times are changing. Our technology is continuously growing. Eric loves technology; he's been using computers since age three. What makes him so unique is that he has not only studied multiple facets of online strategies, but has spent much of his time working in that field. He has worked alongside many business owners, CEOs, sports legends, celebrities, as well as major heads of television, radio, and film.

Watching Eric continue to accomplish wonders has been phenomenal to watch. After a short time, he had gained millions of viewers. Not bad for someone new to the business. He went on to enhance his eZWay brand, which at the time had no momentum. Hundreds of film, business, and sports stars have given eZWay a shout-out from numerous red carpets.

I am in awe of how much he does. He works long hours, makes endless phone calls, spends hours doing online technical work, and at the end of it all, he always adds another creation to his ever-expanding network. As soon as I'm ready to relax and celebrate, he's back on the phone planning his next business venture.

Eric has created various eZWay entities under eZWayBroadcasting and EZWayNetwork TV, including promotions, events, business consulting, development, live stream and social media, Radio, Television, Magazines, Speaking and there will always be more…

Eric's most precious creation is eZWayCares, a nonprofit that has supported and helped numerous nonprofits with the potential to global assistance.

Eric works very well with people. He extends friendship and support to his media competitors. Some of them have gone on to become eZWay affiliates, such as Actors Reporter, Fan TV, Soul Central TV/Magazine, and Film On (powered by Verizon), which distributes to Roku, Amazon Fire, FanTV, Apple TV, Viacom, Comcast, and numerous other networks, channels and affiliate relationships.

Eric is paving the way into the digital age. He has, as many would agree, become somewhat of a portal in this transition, thanks to his expertise in branding and marketing. The buzz, in and out of the boardroom, is that when you want the best, you look for Eric Zuley. He has millions of confirmed connections and is followed by over 47,000 corporations. There are thousands of people waiting to watch his next move, in the hopes that they can incorporate his ideas into their business.

I just want to share who Eric is, as well as all the compassion and hard work happening behind the scenes. His average workday starts at 7am and lasts until 11pm, six days a week (with half a day on Sunday). He's not afraid to share his love for God on his shows, and is frequently seen wearing a hat that reads, "I Love Jesus."

The amount of love and support Eric receives is inspiring. The online eZWayFam comprises of so many good people, many of whom we see at various live events. These individuals have been with us a long time and have become like family.

Eric has many fervent supporters, and I want to let them know how much he and I both appreciate that support. I thank all of you so much for the love you've given my son. God bless you all.

About James Zuley

James Zuley was born in a suburb west of Chicago, where he attended Catholic school with his three brothers. He attended Wilbur Wright Jr. College and Triton Jr. College.

In 1970, James enlisted in the US Army and was accepted into the Military Police. After receiving an Honorable Discharge, he was accepted into the Hillside Fire Department as a full-time firefighter/ EMT.

After James left the fire department, he returned to college. He moved out to California where he graduated from Santa Ana Jr. College. He went on to Cal State Fullerton to study Psychology and Special Education, which propelled him into the Fostering Children World. After University, James purchased and built several businesses and joint investments in Real Estate in the North Gulf Coast of Florida. A lesson to be learned is to not put your eggs in one basket. He met a woman named "KATRINA" (Hurricane) and she changed his life. As he taught his son, remain resilient and keep moving forward. His son Eric, started his own business, eZWayBroadcasting, which James later joined.

Some of his recent accomplishments and honors include, Front Cover of Hollywood Weekly Magazine, show cased at Warner Bros. Studios. Recipient of the Best Parent Award presented by The Family Film Awards and also, the recipient of the eZWay Legend Award, Faith Conquers All.

He is a co-host with Reatha Gray on eZWay Radio Boomers Live Show. Reatha Gray was the co-host with Betty White on "Off Their Rockers". He is a member of Knights of Columbus, an organization that supports women and children. He supports the Disabled American Veterans Association, as well as many other veteran organizations.

He supports and works with the Founder of Better Visions for Children. He is responsible for raising Eric to become the man that he has. Today, he continues to work with eZWayBroadcasting, and is doing it the eZWay!

Chapter 5

Dr. Dante Sears

I met Eric in a very unorthodox way. It was 2016, and I was building my TV network, Dynamic Alignment Neuro-Transformative Entertainment; DANTE TV - TV for the Higher Mind.

I was focused on a couple goals. One: setting up a positive-impact brand including a TV network based upon neuro-transformative programming (TV that elicits positive behavioral modifications and improves the viewer's life). And two: I was determined to attract my soul mate. I made a list of the top 14 qualities I wanted in a soulmate, and I prayed for God to deliver my mate.

As they say, be careful what you wish for, because you might just get it! Meaning, if you want a loving mate, that loving heart was produced by certain family conditions. For example, a man who is extremely family-oriented will also be very close to his parents. I requested that my mate be family-oriented, God-loving, tender-hearted with me, and have an above-average drive to succeed.

I knew my mate was someone who would be very bright, and would stand apart from his peers due to his unique abilities. He would be someone who experienced success early in life, as well as experiencing humbling setbacks that required my intervention as a healer. I also discerned that this person was someone who was a great strategist and had fostered this success by playing video games in his youth. He would be a couple years younger than me, but very mature for his age.

I consider myself to be a master at manifesting. When I decide I want something, the doors of Heaven open to provide it. This is a major gift from our heavenly parent, because it is an extremely spiritual process.

So, there I was, asking God for this soulmate to come. Five years in Los Angeles made me realize that only God could bring my perfect match, and I was counting on him to deliver.

Not only did God, himself, hook us up, but everyone in town referred me to Eric. At least fifty people asked me if I knew Eric Zuley, or told me I reminded them of him. As I went about my life and business, I would tell people my plans to change the world through television, and the person I was talking to would always say the same things: "Have you met Eric Zuley? You sound just like him."

Boy, was I intrigued! Who was this Eric Zuley guy? I asked the CEO of my networking group, and he just laughed and said, "Oh, he's really good but we can't work with him."

"What does that mean?" I asked.

"Well, he's too good."

"So why aren't we working with him?"

"He makes everyone sign a contract and we can't work with his contacts for 3 years. There's no point."

This Eric guy sounded like a pretty interesting, smart guy. I love business contracts, and by this point, 55 people had told me I reminded them of Eric.

You would think that would be enough for me to have reached out to this guy, but I didn't. I was in a state of flux with that particular networking group, and as I moved away from them, I wasn't certain I wanted to be involved with anyone else that might be attached to that group. So I left the group, and I did not contact Eric Zuley.

Here's where it gets interesting. Months later, I'm on a date, when the guy pulls the car over, just a block from my house and says, "I can't take it anymore."

"What?" I ask, perplexed.

"You're not supposed to be with me, you're supposed to be with Eric Zuley, he said.

"What? Who is this Eric Zuley guy? Why does everyone keep saying that?" I was very flustered, to say the least.

"Eric Zuley!" he said, pulling out his phone. *"Look.* This is your guy. He looks like your ex, and he is clearly your type."

At this point, it completely bewildered me. I looked down at his phone to see the video playing of a blonde-haired guy hosting an outdoor turkey drive for Thanksgiving. As the guy began to talk, and I looked into his eyes, I knew my date was right. This guy was my type. But I said, "No, that guy is not my type. Why does everyone keep saying that?"

"He is. I know you're supposed to be with him," he reiterated.

What a strange thing for your date to say. I was in complete denial and didn't say anything else, except to ask for him to take me home. I denied any attraction to this Eric guy, and I did not make any moves to contact him.

But at the same time, I was starting to get really curious who this guy was. Despite my curiosity, I didn't contact Eric right away. It wasn't until a year later that I made the move and contacted Eric, after yet another wave of people telling me how much I reminded them of him.

I appealed to God one morning. "God, you still haven't brought me my match." God asked me what I was doing to allow the mate to catch up with me. When you manifest someone, your only job is to speak up and say "hi" to them, which I had avoided doing with Eric!

I suddenly realized that the work life I was living would never lead to a successful marriage, let alone relationship - or even dates. I worked from home twelve hours a day, six days a week, chasing my goals and setting up my empire. There was no time for true love to develop, I realized, and very little chance of even meeting my match when I'm mostly working alone.

I asked God to show me the way and, to my chagrin, he said 'What about Eric Zuley? You can't skip Eric Zuley'.

"What?! That guy is stuck in the entertainment world!" I said. "I want out of that scene. I want someone who will appreciate me. That guy will take me for granted. Let's just skip Eric Zuley."

But God said, "You cannot skip Eric Zuley. It is your destiny, and you will find your husband through him."

That was all the motivation I needed. When God says you'll get what you want by doing what he says, you make it happen. So, with tears in my eyes, I finished my prayer. Before I knew what I was doing, I picked up my phone and went on Facebook to look Eric up.

I watched one of his videos and this time, I saw his eyes. He seemed so confident, but the angel in me knew he needed my help. I could see it in his eyes. There was something good there. God told me Eric needed my help to heal. Being the dutiful servant I was, I messaged Eric, and saw that he had already messaged me nearly a year prior, inviting me to connect with his company, eZWayBroadcasting.

He was all business at first, which I appreciated, but we started connecting and next thing I knew, we were on messenger for three hours! He suggested we speak on the phone, and we talked about another three hours. We had the same goals and so much in common that we were finishing each other's sentences. We both seemed to realize we had walked a lot of the same path. It was absolutely magical.

We decided to meet for our first date on Valentine's Day, since we were both so wrapped up in our work that neither of us had bothered to cultivate a Valentine's date. I even requested we meet before the date, so it wouldn't be awkward, but I chickened out of going and God had to remind me or his plan. So, we met on our Valentine's Date - at the movies - and the rest is history.

After a few months of dating, I started helping him grow his budding organization through my company, World Prosperity Network. I began to start helping Eric's business by developing websites, producing shows and commercials, creating marketing materials, developing clear, communicative content, and consulting and contributing my ideas to help him grow his dream empire and expand the eZWayFam.

I've been privileged to help him heal the distracting health issues that were holding him back from pursuing his business goals at full strength. When Eric's beloved father was diagnosed with Lymphoma Cancer again, I sprang into action to make certain he would pull through and made natural medicines to kill the cancer cells and put his body back into remission. I knew Eric wouldn't be his best unless his father was okay, so I gave it my all to help him heal.

I've been so proud to watch Eric grow as a man and as an entrepreneur. The person he is today is like a dream come true. He is my best friend. We are developing products, services, and relationships around the world through our respective brands.

Since I started doing it the eZWay, I've met and gotten to know a few more celebrities that are Eric's friends, such as Tim Brown, Kate Linder, Reatha Grey (*Betty White's Off Their Rockers*), Ken Davitian (*Borat*), Jim Zuley (*Radio Boomers*), Ro Brooks (*The Have and Have Nots*, OWN), and Andy McPhee (*Sons of Anarchy*). I'm also featured on Wire and Getty Images, who sent a photographer to the launch episode of my TV show, *Kiss and Tell with Dante Sears*, to publish our images on their sites. Eric helped me get 3 celebrity guests for the show, executive produced the episode, and helped me close my sponsors. I've been on the cover of Soul Central Magazine, thanks to Eric's amazing 'relationship equity', as he calls it. Not to mention the countless events I've attended. In fact, if it wasn't for eZWay inviting me to exclusive events, I wouldn't have met my partners for the two resort projects I'm developing in Texas and Fiji.

Eric and I co-created 'eZWay Fam', which is an affectionate term we created for his followers. We've done the fun things, like a late night call-in show on Facebook Live

The best part for me of 'doing it the eZWay' is that I get to work alongside my best friend, soulmate, and counterpart.

Dr. Dante's Tips for Success

1. Never say 'no' to your dreams. If you want it, go for it.
2. Speak kindly and motivationally to yourself. Say "You Can Do It", "If not me, who?", If they can, why not me?" Never listen to the person saying you can't do something you want.
3. Relationships are key to success. Treat everyone like they are worth $1,000,000 or more.
4. Health is WEALTH. You cannot be wealthy if you are unhealthy. Always live in the state of ease. Let go of failures, blame, disappointment and forgive EVERYONE - including yourself.
5. Follow up and follow through. Money responds to action, and people love predictability for buying and sales.
6. You are what you eat. Be mindful of what goes in and what comes out of your mouth. Eat an organic, plant-based diet for best results in health, wealth, and lifestyle. There's a rea-

son many of the world's wealthiest people are incredibly health-conscious.

7. Never follow "the rules". Learn the laws and guidelines–always stay well within your integrity - but then draw your own rules.

8. Never underestimate the power of God. Becoming wealthy is a spiritual experience. The same energy that powers you and lives within you is the same energy in those you want to help so you can succeed. Call upon that power, and if you have the integrity to attract goodness, you will soon overflow with positive, happy, supportive clientele that will support your goodwill as long as you maintain your integrity. Pray that God will be with you and bring those who can help you so you may help them and receive what you.

9. To become wealthy, don't work. If you work, don't spend all the money you earn on living expenses. Create jobs. Make other people wealthy. Make your money work for you. Use part of your income to leverage underperforming world currencies for passive payouts 3-10xs your money - and spend that money. I used this technique to multiply my work efforts and become a multi-millionaire in my early 20s. Want to learn how? Text WEALTHY to 55678 for a free gift.

About Dr. Dante Sears

Dr. Dante Sears, 'The Global SOULutions', is a serial entrepreneur and ten-time certified Metaphysical Doctor dedicated to improving the world through conscious business practices. She is the founder and CEO of World Prosperity Network, LUXRE ESTATES, MyPod Resorts, and Prosperibly, the Profit-Share Directory. Dante is also the COO of eZWay Network, host of *Kiss and Tell with Dante Sears*, and co-host of *eZ Talk Live*, to name a few. She helps entrepreneurs reverse terminal, genetic, and incurable diseases and dysfunction – from their life and business - within 30 days, in a process she calls 'Dante's Intervention'. She applies this holistic approach to organizations struggling to turn their businesses into profitable brands.

A gifted communicator and adept problem solver, she specializes in strategic negotiations, business development, and green energy/ wellness real estate development. For over 15 years she has imported goods from 5 continents and 37 countries around the world and she is a talented financial trend forecaster. She is involved in a project to bring green energy, healthy housing, and holistic commerce to developing nations around the world.

Dante is a Heartpreneur; an entrepreneur that designs SOULutions for all humanity. Her jewelry line, Dante Bella, is a designer line of Semi-Precious Stone Therapy Jewelry that not only improves your health, but gives the wearer confidence, clarity, and positive emotions to help them succeed. Learn more about Dr. Dante Sears @: DanteSears.com.

Chapter 6

Sharon Lechter

"Next-Level Success with Sharon Lechter"
by Ian Glover

Renowned author and former CPA, Sharon Lecther is also a speaker, entrepreneur and transformational motivator. The advice she has given, the lessons she has taught, and the lives she has changed have turned her into an icon.

Sharon's methodologies began as a young girl. She had an admiration for math and science, which set a course for a life of focus and discipline. As she began to excel in both fields, she cultivated dreams of becoming a math teacher. Her love of math and biology led her on a double-track for both in college.

Ultimately she chose the four-year path in accounting, which prevented her from pursuing an eight to ten-year stint in genetics.

Working as a CPA taught her how companies either succeeded or failed.

Financial literacy became her strength. She wrote several bestselling books, her vast wealth of knowledge and experience filling hundreds upon hundreds of pages. When someone starts selling that many books, institutions invite that person to speak, and Sharon Lecther quickly became known as a renowned speaker.

She believes a person's message is what makes for a great speaker. "It's not what you say, but how you say it." She emphases being number one in whatever your field is, as well as learning from a mentor who is invested in you. The message is key, and she shares how important it is that your message benefits people.

About seven years ago, she lost her son and thought about retiring from the business world and retreating into a more mellow lifestyle. That didn't last long. Instead, a new fire ignited inside her, and she felt herself being guided towards new heights. She saw the opportunity to use her newfound energy to change the world for the better.

"Sometimes you have to close one door for another to open," she explained, when revealing that she was leaving one of her greatest projects, "Rich Dad Poor Dad." Being recognized for her contribution to the world she was asked to work within two presidential administrations (the Bush and Obama administrations).

Sharon's underlying goal is to empower people to take control of their financial lives and she has a special heart-centered initiative helping women. She is concerned with the ways women handicap and talk down to themselves, and dedicates herself to giving them the confidence they've been looking for. They tend to not take time for themselves. Sharon speaks of a prevailing lack of clarity, focus, passion, and motivation in many women's lives, and that these feelings must be conquered if women are to change the courses of their history.

THE INFLUENCE EFFECT   ERIC J. ZULEY

"It's time to play big," Sharon says. "Live your legacy! It is something that is owed to your children." She knows life doesn't wait for anyone, and most people will regret the chances they don't take.

Sharon is a transformational motivator, and she leads with experience, knowledge, and faith. She is an affluent messenger of hope showing us success is within our grasp, and it is only one website away.

Cherry Creek Lodge

Sharon owns a secluded ranch for those who require solace, adventure, and a rebooting of inspirational creativity. It is hidden in the scenic Arizona forest and lies on forty acres of undisturbed land. This small slice of Heaven has been known to inspire, delight, and motivate all who attend. She invites anyone who needs a getaway to refocus, rejuvenate, and reclaim their genius. There is no room service and no cell service - it truly is an opportunity to rediscover your true self.

Sharon originally wanted the ocean, but her husband wanted the mountains, so they purchased their own private haven equipped with a man-made lake dubbed "Lake Sharon." Sharon refers to the lake as her "miniature ocean." It is fully stocked with bass, Georgia Giant Perch, and crappie. These fish are catch-and-release.

This resort offers fishing, archery, hunting, and hiking, just to name a few of its many amenities. You can do these things while soaking in rustic Old West scenery. You will explore your innocence again and disappear into yourself, erasing any pains and elevating yourself to a new and more profound frequency.

It's a perfect area for artists. Enjoy the paddle boats, UTV tours, skeet shooting and nature expeditions, or simply find inspiration in the divine labyrinth Sharon constructed. It is a labyrinth designed to ensure your symbiotic relationship with this archetypal terrain. Serenity is food for the brain, and you can find it at Cherry Creek Lodge.

There are getaway packages of all types, so find the option that best suits your needs, and enjoy. Check out their website at www.cherrycreeklodge.com.

At eZWayBroadcasting, we recognize the digital sphere we all participate in, as well as the global economy that drives it. We will continue to align ourselves with Sharon Lecther and like-minded, next-level game changers in order to empower you. Educating the global community on the nuances of new technologies will always remain our top focus.

Chapter 7

Kelly Bennett

Kelly had seen Mr. Zuley at numerous events for many years, but for some reason, never decided to pull that networking trigger. Maybe it was because of those jealous naysayers again! Maybe it was because the people Kelly was talking to were Eric's competition, or because Eric wore so many hats? Maybe it was because Eric was a leader who didn't care what negative things people thought of him.

Well, fast forward a couple years, when a friend of Eric's (Mikey Adam Cohen) invited Kelly to one of Eric's client's events. Kelly arrived at the red carpet, saw many cameras and celebrities, and things being run properly. She was impressed and asked who was in charge of the red carpet event, and of course, the answer was...eZWay Promotions' own Eric Zuley!

Eric was summoned, and the two connected again. Kelly saw Mr. Zuley differently and gave him her card. Mr. Zuley, knowing he needed a PR person of his own, called Kelly. The two decided to work together, and now Kelly runs her own PR in collaboration with eZWay Promotions. She holds the title of PR Director and personal PR for Mr. Zuley himself.

"Never Give Up, Give Out, or Give in"
Life Lessons from My Mother,
By Kelly Bennett

I believe our path in life is determined by the decisions we make. My mother taught me that if you fall down, just get up, dust yourself off, and keep going.

My mom was born to a poor, alcoholic family during the Depression. Her dad ran out of money for drinks and made her dance on bar tables at 4 years of age doing the "hoochi coochie" to pay his tab.

She walked barefoot to school and had barely enough to eat. She went to the local orphanage often to survive. When she couldn't eat or get taken care of, she had a solution of her own: If you don't like what you have, change it.

She went to business college to get out of poverty. After graduation she landed a great job typing. She loved to dance, too. She went to the Arthur Murray Dance Studio to take lessons. They hired her to teach instead.

In 1944, she was the first woman locally enlisted in the Marine Corps. Her commanding officer tried to break her down, but she never quit. When she put her mind to something, she finished it. She didn't let others get in her way. After boot camp, she was asked where she wanted to go, and she chose El Toro, California.

The women's barracks weren't finished so they shipped her to the base in Miramar. She partied and danced. She had fun while she could, making every moment count, even while she waited for something else to start.

At El Toro, she wanted to work on airplanes, but instead, she worked as a secretary, coordinating housing for incoming Marines. At the El Toro Marine Base pool, she met a handsome lifeguard named Pete. She soon became pregnant with my older brother. The Marines told her to marry "that Marine," or else get dishonorably discharged. Two years later, another boy was born, and then eleven years later, I was born.

My mother and father were married for 56 years, until my dad died in 2000. When she finally went to a senior dance, she met Dale, a man 10 years younger, who loved her unconditionally. They danced 3-4 times a week. They were inseparable. My mother accepted what life was giving her, and she was grateful for a second chance at love.

She broke her ankle in October 2015, and I moved in to care for her. I got her back on her feet by May 2016. She and Dale then went to the famous Senior Prom. They had so much fun, and it was nice to know my job was done. Enjoy your time you have with your parents. I was lucky I did, and I'm thankful for that.

Dale tended to her needs while I kept the house running. She loved people, and she'd talk to folks everywhere. She'd see everyone's head down looking at their devices and say, "I don't compute!" Go out and meet someone face to face. Have a conversation with your neighbor, the checker at the grocery store or even your own family.

In September 2018, she awoke to find the left side of her face fallen, I immediately called 911. Doctors said it was Bell's Palsy. They discovered she had Non-Hodgkin's Lymphoma and if not treated, she'd live only three more months at most. We opted out of treatment. Quality of life wouldn't be the same. Celebrating her 97th birthday was the goal. Life is fragile. Do the things you want with those you want to do them with, before you no longer can.

She loved hugs. She had every senior at the dances hugging. She knew how important hugging was, how much it enriched the human soul, so she made an effort to show everyone around her how much she cared.

Dale's health started to decline. Dancing stopped, but they still talked for hours. When Dale died in November 2018, it seemed Mom's spirit died as well. Make every second count. We are not guaranteed tomorrow.

It's been 6 months and mom's health is getting worse. We've called in Hospice to keep her comfortable and out of pain. At the time I'm writing this, it is now July 4, 2019. I am watching her decline. July 5, 2019 - I call the family as now it's just a matter of time. July 6, 2019 - the nurse says she has hours left. July 7, 2019 - 8:08pm she is gone. Surround yourself with loved ones and say the things that matter to the people who matter most. Don't wait until it's too late.

My mother taught me to love people for who they are, forgive your past and make today count. My mom lived her life with passion and now, so am I.

About Kelly Bennett

A 20-year award-winning broadcast journalist, Kelly Bennett has been a reporter, anchor, TV host, Radio Host, senior assignment manager before transitioning into public relations managing community affairs for two Fortune 500 companies. In 2009, she founded Bennett Unlimited PR, giving her clients local, national and international notoriety. She connects clients to influencers to further their goals. She created Purpose Driven PR, which provides online support through videos, webinars, events, and masterminds, consisting of experts guiding people "How to Unleash the Power of Media to Launch or Grow Your Mission-Driven Business".

www.PurposeDrivenPR.com

Chapter 8

Frank Shankwitz

I met Eric through an association, Allison Hildebrandt Larsen of the Speaker's Coalition. We were on the same board of that organization. When we met in person, Eric interviewed me for the movie *Wish Man* at the Spirit Summit. In this unique interview, I took Eric's hat off, removed mine, then put his hat on my head. He just laughed, and was very approachable and friendly. This was the first interview including both myself and Andrew Steel who played Frank in my movie, *Wish Man*. It was the beginning of a great friendship. Since then, we've collaborated on many events and he has included me on the Wall of Fame. It has been great to watch the growth of, and feel the tremendous support from, the eZWay family.

About Frank Shankwitz

Frank Shankwitz is best known as the creator, co-founder, and first president/CEO of the Make-A-Wish Foundation, an extraordinary charity that grants wishes to children with life-threatening illnesses. From humble beginnings, the Make-A-Wish Foundation is now a global organization that grants a new child's wish on an average of every 28 minutes.

Frank is a U.S. Air Force veteran, and has a long and distinguished career in law enforcement. He began as an Arizona Highway Patrol Motorcycle Officer and retired as a Homicide Detective with the Arizona Department of Public Safety, with 42 years of service.

Frank has been featured in many publications and television programs. He has received several awards, including the White House Call to Service Award from both President George W. Bush and President Donald J. Trump, as well as the "Making a Difference in the World" Award from the U.S. Military Academy at West Point.

In 2015, Frank joined six U.S. presidents, Nobel Prize winners, and industry leaders as a recipient of the Ellis Island Medal of Honor. In December of that year, following his commencement address, they presented Frank with an Honorary Doctorate Degree, Doctor of Public Service, from The Ohio State University. Frank was identified as one of the "10 Most Amazing Arizonans", in a front-page article in the *Arizona Republic* newspaper.

In January 2016, Frank was identified in a *Forbes* article as a "*Forbes* Top Ten Keynote Speaker."

In April 2017, he was presented the Unite4: Humanity Celebrity ICON Social Impact Award, joining past recipients Matthew McConaughey and Morgan Freeman.

In February 2018, Frank shared the stage with Matthew McConaughey at Universal Studios at the LA City Gala, where he presented the first City Gala Hero Award. Frank's new book *Wish Man* was re-released in September 2018, and is available on Amazon.

In May 2019, following his commencement address, Frank was presented with an Honorary Doctorate Degree, Doctor of Law, from St. Norbert College.

In June 2019, Frank joined 89 celebrities when he received his "STAR" on the Las Vegas Walk of Fame. Frank's life story, *Wish Man,* is a major motion picture released that same month.

Frank is a board member on several nonprofit organizations, including U.S. Vets, The Wounded Blue, and Broadway Hearts. To contact Frank for a speaking engagement, go to his website - wishman1.com.

Chapter 9

Shea Vaughn

Today I am known as a lifestyle pioneer, broadcast network CEO, bestselling author, producer, and I am nationally recognized as a wellness authority. My life-changing work and philanthropy are endorsed by the City of Chicago and the Department of Public Health. I first earned recognition as "American's Queen of Wellness" by creating SheaNetics, from which I became  a sought-after influencer, an entertaining keynote speaker, and a role model for how positive living can bring joy into someone's life.

As a young, energetic seven-year-old girl, my mom enrolled me in several dance lessons. I was driving my mom crazy doing cartwheels, dancing, and jumping all over the house. Once I began my lessons, I loved every moment spent in the studio.

At nine, they invited me to join a professional performance team. This was even better than I could have imagined! Ballet was the hardest of all the dances I was practicing; it challenges every muscle in your body, even some you never knew you had. Additionally, all professional dance requires commitment to do your best to reach your own personal goals. For me, it helped reinforce my own strength.

Many years later, I was certified in yoga, Tai Chi, Pilates, strength training, and more. I even created my own brand "SheaNetics®" an innovative value-based, doctor-endorsed lifestyle practice that enhances the quality of one's physical, nutritional, mental and emotional intelligence, using the winning power of its transformational "SheaFit" programs and SheaNetics grounding 5 Principles of Wellness. These principles are commitment, perseverance, self-control, integrity and love.

SheaNetics® has written the next chapter in fitness by creating its own breakthrough SheaFit multi-discipline workouts. They are a one-of-a-kind mash-up of yoga exercises, Pilates, mixed martial arts, dance, GYROKENISIS® and more. Noted for their constant variety, incredible effectiveness SheaNetics Tri-Core-Power Training helps you achieve a "killer core."

SheaNetics workouts deliver a challenging and dynamic innovation in body performance exercise that is multi-age-suitable for any fitness level.

But how did a "fitness queen" create a TV network? Well, the first step began some years ago in Chicago. I was beyond grateful when I was asked to be a TV contributor to four major TV networks: ABC's Windy City Live, Fox, NBC and CBS. I would be speaking on fitness and wellness. It was during this period I decided I wanted to host my own show. I got close to making this happen twice, but to my disappointment, it just never came together. All of this made me take a step back and ask myself, "Why?"

It was at this time that I did some research and found several other amazing women who would have loved to have hosted their own TV show. But at the time, there wasn't much of a demand for female television hosts. I began researching what it would take to build my own television network specifically for women. I wanted to learn how to give women a voice, and provide them a platform to spread their messages worldwide.

With the help of my husband, Steve, we found an IT company in Chicago that helped us understand what it would take to build such a platform. Fast forward to one year later. We sold our house and moved from Chicago to LA, in order to be with the children (Victoria, Valerie, Vincent) and the grandchildren. This move not only helped us stay connected with the family, but it allowed us to find the right IT partner, Jayne Rios, to build the TV platform.

My dream came true on October 1, 2016, when we launched "Women on TV," the first OTT and online digital TV network with original content specifically targeting women. Sadly, only two years later, Jayne passed away from cancer in the fall of 2018. She will be forever missed and especially by John Rios, her loving husband, as well as her mother and her two young sons.

Following this tragedy, Steve and I were blessed to find a new IT company, Beck Computer Systems, in Lakewood, CA. They had 35 years of experience in IT solutions, and they offered consulting services tailored to a business' specific needs. Gary Beck and Bruce Kraft were excited about what we were doing. We all agreed they should join the WWTVN team, as its Chief Technology Officer and Chief Media Officer.

They did, and together with our fusion of OTT and technology abilities, Women On TV, as well as our other networks (Direct Sales TV and Worldwide TV Network) are growing and expanding each day. After that, we started work on a podcast network that would give our television hosts access to a larger audience.

We have reached an audience of over forty million people, and through OTT (Over The Top) partners like Roku, AppleTV, and other networks, we are offering viewers and hosts an engaging digital meeting space to connect, collaborate, and communicate with like-minded individuals.

WWTVN is exploiting the explosion in quality and cost-effective digital production of audio/video content. Through my world-class broadcasting networks, aspiring hosts can become influential experts, grow their networks, and build their brands' credibility.

I believe in providing a wide mixture of tools and opportunities to our hosts. I believe through your own faith and love; you have everything you need to be successful. At WWTVN we say, "You don't have to be a celebrity to be a star," and together, we can unite the world.

Meeting Eric Zuley

A few years ago, my husband Steve, along with James Dentley (a leading authority on motivational speaking and a very dear friend), invited me to an "invite-only" event held in Dana Point, California. The event was called Influencers United, and when we got there, the place was filled with people dressed in fashionable attire. They were all laughing having an exceptionally good time, judging by their looks and attitudes. We made our way to our assigned table and sat down to listen to several enthralling speakers, while enjoying a meal.

Dessert followed, and as the music started, everyone was asked to go to the outside deck for the red carpet portion of the evening. I usually take this opportunity to say hello and engage with people. However, this time I wanted to just observe. So I stayed at our table, when only a few minutes later, a tall, well-dressed young man approached me. He was smiling, and he introduced himself as Eric Zuley.

He asked me if I would like to step outside for an interview. How could I say no? Eric reached for my hand and led me outside, into the festive club-like atmosphere. Camera lights were flashing as each influencer moved from one interviewer to the next, sharing their stories about how they got to where they are today.

Eric introduced me to his father, James Zuley. After the interview, Eric and James walked me around the event, enthusiastically introducing me to many amazing people. I met a woman named Allison Larson, an international keynote speaker, mentor, author, and the founder of the Speakers Coalition.

Fast forward a few years, and Eric and I have developed a very unique relationship. I support his efforts, and he supports mine. We've struggled through some of the same childhood challenges, and most of all, we always put family and faith above everything else.

Chapter 10

James Dentley

I met Eric at a prestigious awards event in Los Angeles, California. He and I both were receiving an award that night. I remember his smile, and his quiet, intense demeanor as he introduced himself. He has carried that same friendly, yet focused energy to this day. After many discussions, I have found him to be a visionary, a trendsetter, and a man of integrity. He has invited me on his radio show many times, and has always offered to help me in my times of need. He has become a dependable resource, and an incredible friend.

I have spoken in front of audiences with over 25,000 people, and I've trained over 500,000 people. Both my wife and myself consider ourselves blessed to be working in both the business arena and the nonprofit space. I have worked with politicians, corporate executives, thought leaders, and entrepreneurs throughout the world. The thing my partners have in common is a burning desire to make our world a better place, a passion for inspiring hearts and minds.

As we move into the future, eZWay is expanding its media reach and once again, Eric Zuley, with his warm smile and sincere demeanor, has offered to promote our message on his new streaming network. We are honored to call eZWay not only a partner, but a friend.

About James Dentley

James Dentley is a gentle giant, teaching straight from his heart. His passionate, high-energy concepts bring measurable positive results. He produces his own streaming TV network, radio talk shows, and podcasts. He also works with Limitless Women, "where everything is possible." James runs his organization with his wife Kara Scott Dentley, who is a powerhouse herself, and together they dedicate their efforts to empowering women and bringing services and opportunities to children, veterans, and seniors.

James is an entrepreneur and the bestselling author of *The 5 Frequencies of High Performance*. He is a philanthropist, and remains one of the nation's top life and business strategists. As a motivational speaker, James Dentley is a dynamic personality, and is highly sought after resource in business circles. He works with Fortune 500 CEOs, small business owners, nonprofits and community leaders from all sectors of society looking to expand opportunity. He has trained over 500,000 people, eighty of whom have become millionaires.

In 2008, he founded which is now the #1 speakers and communication program, 'Inspired2Speak: Action Camp. His mission is to empower entrepreneurs and business owners to create massive success and to achieve their dreams. He can "transform good speakers to great speakers and great speakers to legendary." He has spent over two decades working with everyone from start-ups to major global brands, working to help them increase sales, productivity, and overall success. He is an innovator with a remarkable ability to help business owners seize immediate market opportunities. For everyone that owns a business, or would like to capitalize their entrepreneurial dream, his message will provide them with knowledge and principles to turn that passion into a success!

Dentley has addressed audiences from North, South and Latin America, Europe, Asia-Pacific, and the Caribbean. He is invited back again and again, thanks to his powerful message, and his innate ability to connect with people from all walks of life. It isn't just his great smile, humble nature, or his way with words that motivates people; the depth of his knowledge on achievement creates lasting results. He is a frequent speaker on the Think and Grow Rich Tour, as well as a trusted partner with the OG Mandio Business Institute. He also works with CEO Space, the eZWay media company, The City Gala and Summit, and The Executive Club, just to name a few.

Contact information:
www.jd@thejamesdentleyshow.com
www. thejamesdentleyshow.com
www. jamesdentley.com www. inspired2speakto

Chapter 11

Sean Douglas Stewart

I met Eric Zuley at a business growth seminar in 2018. I was immediately impressed after hearing him speak onstage. I couldn't believe the kind of people that he knew, nor could I fathom the kind of access he had. Beyond that, I was impressed with the systems he'd built to help people gain more exposure for their businesses. Once I learned he had a background in music, specifically with hip hop, I knew we were destined to connect.

Since then, I've gotten to know Eric on a deeper level. The thing I admire most about him is his heart. He really cares about people, and truly wants them to become successful. That's the kind of person I've always wanted to work with.

My background is that of a transformational business coach, visibility expert and speaker. I help coaches and entrepreneurs build a fully expressed, high-impact, freedom-based business around their core gifts. I'm the founder of The Creative Track and the creator of Rock

Your Gift LIVE — the first business growth seminar meets conscious hip hop concert.

I run Rock Your Gift TV, I've been featured on NBC, FOX and *The New York Times,* and I've shared stages with some of the biggest leaders in the personal growth industries like Les Brown, Lisa Sasevich, and Shift Network founder Stephen Dinan. I was originally trained by Tony Robbins, and I have a background as a spoken word poet, song-writer and rapper, and I absolutely love inspiring audiences at my live events and workshops.

eZWay has helped me spread my message to more people in a massive way. Eric is consistently putting himself out there, taking action and putting 100% into everything he does. It seems like whenever I go to any event, I can always count on seeing Eric. And sure enough, Eric is always there with his camera crew, interviewing people and creating an atmosphere of buzz and excitement. He surrounds himself with lots of talented and creative people. The value of simply watching Eric work is immeasurable.

Eric has helped my videos get more views, he has promoted several of my programs - there's almost nothing he hasn't done for me, and he'll do the same for all of his clients.

From Sean Douglas Stewart:

Download my "Viral Visibility Checklist," which will show you how to make your social media posts and videos go viral.

Grab the checklist here: https://seanstewart.lpages.co/standoutoptin1

Chapter 12

Hanna Horenstein

I've been an entrepreneur for over 25 years. I began my career at 18, when I worked in the real estate business. I formed my own real estate marketing company before I turned 20. Around 22, I made my way into the financial services industry, and I've kept my flag planted in that business ever since.

I have coached and trained hundreds of people. I discovered my passion was to help others achieve the same type of success I had. My team has been expanding ever since it began, and by now, my company has expanded throughout North America.

I credit the majority of my success to all the great mentors I've been fortunate enough to meet. I've been mentored by some of the top individuals in the financial and insurance industries. I excel in providing support and direction to anyone in the country hoping to achieve financial independence. Some of my clients have included athletes and celebrities, as well as every day, hard-working families and business owners.

I first spotted Eric Zuley speaking on the Think and Grow Rich Legacy World Tour in San Diego. I realized there was something unique about him, and inspired by his words, I introduced myself during the red carpet portion of the evening. One week later, I met with Eric at The Center Club, a private country club. After that meeting, I signed on with eZWay, and immediately, the introductions, advice, and social media heat buzz started growing.

My vision is to bring financial literacy and entrepreneurial opportunities to more and more people, as I feel this industry has changed my life drastically. I would love to tell my story and hopefully inspire others to take the same actions in achieving their own success. I have been able to build my own business (while raising two children), and I would love to share my secrets, in order to make everyone's dream of financial independence come true.

Chapter 13

Gerald L. Kane

I met Eric over the phone, via a conversation with a mutual friend of ours, Denise Millett-Burkhardt. He introduced himself, and we discussed putting together a commercial for the upcoming *Wish Man* movie. Within two hours, the commercial was finished, and it aired that evening. Needless to say, I was impressed how quickly we were able to put that project together.

Since then, Eric has opened the door to many opportunities for me. We created a segment on his radio show *Baby Boomers* called "Baby Boomer Benefits." That segment highlights the legal and financial planning opportunities available for boomers. It also helps veterans understand the financial benefits they're eligible to receive. These benefits provide assistance later in life so veterans (and their spouses) can age with dignity, as well as achieve a higher quality of life, better retirement, and prevents them from outliving their assets.

Eric made connections to the Speaking Empire, giving me a perfect place to present my message. He connected me to Patricia Sadler of New Life Clarity Publishing, and we have written a book that helps veterans apply for, and understand how to, get hidden benefits. Eric also introduced me to his father Jim Zuley, who is in the process of connecting me with more veterans that need help. Denise Millett-Burkhardt is connecting me with her project Vetterlands, which will help me serve even more veterans.

I am thankful to have met Eric, as he has opened the door to more opportunities, and is helping me grow my business. Eric does everything he says he will and more. He is passionate, caring, energetic, and kind. Sometimes I find myself collaborating with him Saturday evenings at midnight, because he's always working and thinking, and he never sleeps.

The Evolution of a Forward-Thinking Lawyer

When my oldest daughter was five, she was officially diagnosed with autism. Before that, doctors simply thought she was bipolar. We knew something was off, because she had difficulty socializing and maintaining eye contact. Teachers kept telling us she was autistic, and for some time, my first wife and I refused to accept we had brought a child into this world who had "problems." Classic denial.

Our second daughter was born two years after our first. My first wife was constantly stressed; she and I simply weren't prepared for the unique challenges raising an autistic child would place on our marriage. My wife was diagnosed with cancer, and after she passed away, I eventually remarried, but my family situation put a strain on the new relationship.

I felt helpless. I had stayed by my ex-wife's side night and day, through every surgery, and I knew I couldn't save her. In addition to taking care of our children, I had become my wife's caregiver as well. Even though I was surrounded by loving family members, I felt completely alone.

But that challenging period taught me something. As a result of those hardships, my life evolved, and so did my practice. I really enjoyed helping people solve their problems, legally and financially. I wanted to help them navigate a very complex system.

For example, as my clients began aging, I became an elder law attorney. Clients would often ask me questions about Medi-Cal planning. I got involved, and I learned how VA Pension could help a tremendous number of veterans get the care they needed.

I also got into Special Needs Planning, because I have a daughter with special needs. I make sure Critical Care Planning is looked into fully, after everything I went through with my first wife. I understand firsthand how these things can spin out of control, and I want to use my unique set of skills and life experiences to help other families. I can help my clients prepare for anything. They can rest assured knowing their finances and well-being are very well taken care of. My expertise has given me the opportunity to not only provide security for my new wife, children, and cats, but also share my knowledge with others.

Some services I offer at my firm in Encino, California:

Estate Planning, Trusts, Trust Administration, Special Needs Planning, Probate, Limited Conservatorships, Conservatorships, Pet Trusts, Medi-Cal Planning, Veterans Benefits, Asset Protection and Preservation.

About Gerald L. Kane

Recognized as a "Super Lawyer" (top 5% of all attorneys), Attorney Gerald L. Kane has helped more than 3,000 businesses and families achieve their business and estate planning goals, while shielding them from estate and income taxes, creditors and probate.

A graduate from the University of LaVerne, College of Law, he is a certified specialist in estate planning, trust and probate law, and has been accredited with the Veteran's Administration. He is a member of Wealth Counsel, a charter member of the American Academy of Special Needs Planners, former trustee of the Granada Hills Hospital Foundation, and a recipient of the American Jurisprudence Award in Wills and Trusts. Gerald is also a recognized speaker and enjoys educating people in finance in law.

He has over 25 years of experience in helping clients plan and prepare for virtually any complications that may arise while protecting their wealth. His financial, real estate, legal training, as well as his real life experience, has helped him grow a successful and innovative practice.

Developing lifelong relationships with his clients is important to him. He ensures business owners are protected from the myriad of legal and tax issues that could arise. He guarantees that the business "lives on" after the founder is gone. He sets families up with solid financial plans to protect their savings and assets.

Gerald has a sincere understanding and compassion for what people struggle with financially, emotionally, and legally. He assists families with special needs planning, critical illness planning, as well as planning for various stages of life, including death. His plans for special needs children ensure they will be protected throughout and beyond their parents' lifetimes. Recently, Gerald's firm expanded to include elder law and veteran's benefits.

Happily married to his beautiful wife, they live in Oak Park with their family of cats. Gerald continues to share his expertise with the world.

Chapter 14

Reatha Grey

After returning from an extended hiatus from show business, I returned to a whole new Hollywood. Headshots were no longer in black and white, reality TV was all the rage, and everyone was attempting to get their fifteen minutes of fame. It was a whole new world. Enter Eric Zuley!

I was attending some event, and this string bean of a man was interviewing people on the red carpet. We met, connected, and that was the beginning of my foray into the eZWay world!

Since then, I have walked dozens of red carpets, interviewed luminaries, co-hosted events, broadcasted live, taped podcasts, met hundreds of different influencers, show biz, and business people, all through my association with Eric. This young man is a powerhouse of energy. Whether it's a large event in a stadium, or an intimate business opening, Eric knows everybody's name and story. I call him the human Rolodex.

Being a part of the eZWay Fam has been a boost to my career. I have been given great networking opportunities. It is an honor to be on the eZWay Wall of Fame. It is a privilege to co-host *Radio Boomers Live* on the eZWay Broadcasting Network. I'm proud to have co-hosted the first eZWay Awards, in association with eZWay Cares. As Eric says, "Why do it the hard way when you can do it the eZWay?"

About Reatha Grey

Reatha Grey is one of the senior pranksters from *Betty White's Off Their Rockers*, the award-winning show that aired for two seasons on NBC and one season on The Lifetime Channel.

Reatha was born in Los Angeles, California, attended Los Angeles High School, Los Angeles City College, and UCLA. After touring with the USO, Reatha began her professional show business career appearing in television series and movies such as *Three's Company, General Hospital,* and *Angel Dusted*. She opened the Grey Images Extra Casting Company, which went on to cast TV shows and movies like *Frank's Place, The Slap Maxwell Story, Baby Boom,* and *I'm Gonna Git You Sucka.*

After an extended hiatus from the entertainment industry between 1991 and 2006, Reatha returned to acting in 2007. She can be seen annually in holiday TV films including Netflix's *Christmas on Salvation Street, A Christmas Cruise,* and *A Husband for Christmas.* She appeared on recent episodes of *Castle, Grace and Frankie, It's Always Sunny in Philadelphia, The Cool Kids,* and three episodes of *The Rich and the Ruthless.*

Reatha received the 2016 NAFCA (Nollywood African Film Critics Award) Best Actress in an Independent Film for *Betrothed*. She co-hosts *Radio Boomers Live*, where she can be heard discussing all things human from a baby boomer's perspective. The podcast airs on the eZWay Broadcasting Network on Mondays at 10am.

You can keep up with Reatha on Facebook, Twitter, Instagram and her website, ReathaGrey.com.

Chapter 15

Trae Ireland

I met Eric through a mutual friend. We were all working together making music videos. That first encounter with Eric led to a meeting in Eric's office, and we became genuine friends, like Muhammad Ali and Howard Cosell. Eric has used eZWay's various platforms to increase awareness of my movies, which has allowed me to receive much more exposure than I would have otherwise. Eric is an amazing human being, and I consider it to be a great privilege and honor to call him a friend.

Here are my 5 Steps to Success:

1. Put GOD first in your life.
2. Maintain a strong work ethic
3. Be careful whom you trust
4. Utilize your resources
5. Dress the part

About Trae Ireland

Trae Ireland began by working with a courier service. He delivered headshots and packages to casting directors. As a result of his daily deliveries and interactions, he developed a rapport with many different casting directors. He asked if there were any roles for him, and to keep him in mind if one opened up.

In 1999, that door of opportunity finally opened. Trae connected with William Allen Young. Mr. Young starred in *Matlock*, *The Jeffersons*, and *Lock Up* (with Sylvester Stallone). At the time, Young was playing Moesha's dad on the hit show *Moesha*. When he met Trae at an awards show in Chicago, Trae asked if it would be possible to visit the set of *Moesha*. Impressed by Trae's upfront and sincere approach, Young gave Trae his contact information.

Once he was in Los Angeles, Trae contacted Young, and was invited to the set. As soon as he stepped onto the set, Trae studied everything. One day, his prayers were answered when he was able to audition for a role, and then the rest is history.

Trae's willpower, drive, motivation, and tenacity is unmatched. His first audition was successful, which led to a recurring role, and this opportunity allowed him to get other roles. Trae's humble heart and determination have helped him succeed in Hollywood. In show business, all a person has is their word, and who they are as a person. Trae lives by the motto: "If you can believe it, you can achieve it."

Chapter 16

Annie McKnight

My journey with Eric began many years ago. I was working as a stand-up comic, actress, and staff writer for BET. I met him one night, at a club in Hollywood. My late former publicist Eugenia Wright arranged the meeting.

As I walked through the door, Eric said, "Hi, Annie McKnight, I'm Eric Zuley, and you're funny." Even back then, he was a businessman at heart. I got to know him, simply because he was everywhere, at all the hottest spots in Los Angeles. Whenever I bumped into him at a club, we always talked. He was in the process of building his public persona, and I remember he was such a ladies' man: tall, slim, blonde, and talkative.

Eric has always been bold, hardworking, and consistent. As the years passed, we both grew into our own as people and performers, and our paths continued to cross. We have always respected one another. I'm so happy I've been able to watch him grow, from that hip young man into a well-groomed suit-and-tie businessman. Eric rocks, and I wish him nothing but the best.

I appreciate his friendship, and his enthusiasm for my comedy. We are currently planning our business venture together; I've been asked to partner with one of his associates to produce some comedy shows for his network. I'm looking forward to many successful years with the eZWay network.

About Annie McKnight

Annie McKnight is an actress, comedienne, and writer. She is definitely a WINNER! In 2018, she was the winner of the HAPA awards. Her quick, provocative, and clever wit has taken her from New York City's hottest comedy clubs to all the hottest comedy clubs in California.

Her extensive list of credits includes Martin Lawrence's *First Amendments*, writing jobs for BET, Team Coco, as well as personal appearances on the *Melody Trice Show*. She guest-starred in *The Soloist, Cornered*, and *Crazy On the Outside* (starring Tim Allen).

More information on MCfunny checkout her website Annie-Mcknight.com, IG: _@mcfunny. She can be found on Facebook and Twitter.

Chapter 17

Nay Nay Kirby

Nay Nay first met Eric Zuley in Beverly Hills, when he was hosting a fundraiser against bullying called the "STOP TOUR." It was an amazing red carpet event, with plenty of stars and press! Nay Nay worked as an actress in a film about bullying, which was screened at that same event. Eric recognized her talent, and since then, he has remained friends with both Nay Nay and her mother Monique.

Nay Nay's Formula for Success:

1. Pray
2. Remain Humble
3. Network
4. Industry Relationships are extremely important. Do not take them for granted.
5. Promote and invest in yourself

About Nay Nay Kirby

Born in Northern California, Nay Nay Kirby started her career in San Francisco, booking print jobs and commercials at the tender age of 4. She currently resides in Los Angeles and is now 17 years old.

Her credits include:

- 2013 Little Miss African American Pageant Scholarship Queen, producer Lisa Ruffin.
- Nay Nay is an acting assistant for Mr. Kiko Ellsworth. She teaches Improv, scene study, and cold reading for children ages 7 to 12
- She has been the Children's Ambassador for the Annual Leimert Park Village Book Fair since 2012
- She is the creator and designer of teen pajamas, onesies and two pieces called "Kirby Couture"
- She's been featured in over 40 Music Videos with A-list Award Winning Artists such as

Jill Scott, "Lovely Day"

Akon, "Akon Drops"

Akon featuring Michael Jackson, "Hold my Hand"

Eddie Murphy and Snoop Lion, "Red Light"

- Nay Nay is a trained tap dancer under the instruction of Mr. Chester Whitmore
- She has co-starred in two episodes on the Nickelodeon TV Show *100 Things Before High School*
- Nay Nay was the "2015 BEST ACTRESS" Award Winner at the Las Vegas Film Festival

Nay Nay is a screenwriter, a member of ASCAP AND SAG (Screen Actors Guild). She is also a radio show host, rapper, songwriter, show producer, and model. She is also a Disney Official YouTube Channel host and producer of *Descendants Pop Talk*, alongside costume designer Kara Sean.

Chapter 18

Jeff Levine

I'm a former tax attorney and certified financial planner. All my clients were business owners, and as they approached their retirement years, they eventually wanted to retire from their businesses. So I helped them. I laid out a plan, a business plan, so that they could become more profitable. And when they sold their businesses, every one of my clients had something substantial to sell.

I met Eric Zuley at the WFG Wealth Ball in Palm Springs, CA. He was as friendly as a person could be, and I was excited; I could feel the energy in the room, everybody's walking the red carpet, cameras are flashing, and all of the sudden, I'm being interviewed. It was incredible, and he introduced me to a lot of influential people.

When my movie premiered at Universal Studios, I asked Eric to help me out with the red carpet, and he said he had a publicist for me. It was such a special experience, walking the red carpet at my own movie premiere, being interviewed, and getting the opportunity to speak about my experiences. I've been an active participant in Eric's magazine, I've been to several different industry events, I've got a spot on the Wall of Fame, and it's all thanks to Eric.

Eric runs with an incredible crowd. I'm meeting top-notch people that I normally would not have had the opportunity to meet. Eric has a seemingly endless amount of friends and connections, and this gives me a chance to influence many more people. He's giving me a chance to really spread my message. It gives me an opportunity to share my influence with and work closely alongside Eric. It's refreshing to have a really tight-knit working relationship with someone.

You will find the Wealth Builder's Channel that has been created for ROKU on the eZWay Broadcasting network and see all the things that I will be creating with Eric. Above all, I'm just striving to be a better influencer. I have to be. When you're working with Eric, you're working with the best, and you either meet his standard, or you go home. I am doing it the eZWay.

About Jeffrey Levine:

Jeffrey Levine is a highly skilled Tax Planner and Business Strategist, as well as a published author, and sought-after speaker. He's been featured in national magazines, on the cover of Influential People Magazine, and a frequent featured expert on radio, talk shows, and documentaries. Mr. Levine attended the prestigious Albany Academy for High School, and then went on to University of Hartford at Connecticut, University of Mississippi Law School, Boston University School of Law, and earned an L.L.M. in Taxation. His accolades include features in both Kiplinger and Family Circle Magazine, as well as a dedicated commentator for both Channel 6 and 13 news shows, a contributor for the Albany Business review, and an announcer for WGY Radio.

Mr. Levine has accumulated over 30 years-experience as a Tax Attorney and Certified Financial Planner and has given over 500 speeches internationally. Mr. Levine's curriculum is centered around professional and personal development and as co-founder of the Carnegie Principle Education. Jeffrey's lifelong mission is to give back to people in need by coaching them to utilize the resources they have available to meet or exceed their desired objectives. Mr. Jeffery Levine is the executive producer and cast member in the upcoming documentary, ***Beyond the Secret, The Awakening***.

Mr. Levine's most current work ***Consistent Profitable Growth Map,*** is a step by step workbook outlining easy to follow steps to convert consistent revenue growth to any business platform. He and his team are dedicated to helping you and your organization achieve your ultimate tax strategy and profitable business exit.

Chapter 19

Amy K Thomson

As I write this, I am already a successful performer, with my books, programs, website, clothing line, and TV Show in the works. I have also recently started working with the New Life Clarity Publishing team, formatting books (I'm formatting this book, in fact). Things have been both exciting and challenging. Most people would attribute their success to just 'being in the right place at the right time', but that's pretty much never the case.

For those of you who don't know me, I've had an interesting past. Some might call it turbulent. Others would call it adventurous, enlightening, fun, sad, or perhaps interesting. Pretty much any adjective you could think of would fit, as I've been through things most people would never dream of.

But I'm optimistic, in spite of those traumas. People tend to think my optimism means I'm completely oblivious to anything bad that could happen. They think all I see is sunshine and lollipops, but that's not true. I've just experienced enough negativity to know it's healthier for me to see obstacles as opportunities.

I've been diagnosed with schizotypal personality disorder. I've also been diagnosed with bipolar disorder, depression, anxiety, ADHD, and a few others. But it's not all bad. Every adversity comes with its own hidden gifts and opportunities. For example, I am extremely empathetic, and I'm very in tune with energy.

I didn't always look at my struggles as a positive thing. I used to believe my mental health issues meant I would never have the ability to achieve my goals. I used to feel like a victim, helpless to my illnesses. I believed something was "wrong with me," meaning I was less than everyone around me.

But obviously, this is untrue. I'm not less than, and anyone who struggles with some of these same challenges is, of course, not less than anyone else. I firmly believe these challenges are blessings in disguise, and I've developed a few different self-empowerment programs to help people come to the same realizations I have.

For example, my Affirming Arts™ combines personal development with creative arts. It helps people feel good, become empowered, and take control of their lives. My Finisher's Club™ program and planning system helps people organize their thoughts, notice opportunities, make plans, track details and achieve results.

Finally, my 30 Days to Happiness program helps people realize their happiness and accept who they truly are, regardless of external conditioning and expectations. The program has helped many people build habits for lasting happiness and success.

People often tell me how grateful they are that I can be happy with pretty much anything that happens. As it turns out, optimism is contagious. Taking on life with mental health issues can be pretty overwhelming. There are a lot of feelings to manage, but I've found that as long as I remain focused on feeling a little better each day, things will continue to improve.

Most importantly, I give myself permission to fail. Simply put, I allow myself to be me, regardless of what mood I'm in.

I'm happy to report I rarely hide out now, (although periodically, I still have rough days). I am working with people, trusting them more than I used to, and most of all, I'm trusting life. I've put my faith at the forefront, and I expect everything to work out for the best.

Which brings me to Eric Zuley. Eric is a man of tremendous faith, and for a while, before I'd even met him, many people on social media kept asking if I knew him, or what I thought of him. I ignored those messages, as I sometimes find managing social media to be overwhelming. I thought if I jumped at every chance to meet every suggested friend, then I would just be adding more distractions to my life.

Thanks to some encouragement from some very awesome people (Teresa Snider, Pattie Sadler, Jeremiah Knight), I ended up meeting Eric. He interviewed me on his father's radio show. It was an experience I greatly enjoyed; both Jim and his co-host Reatha were simply amazing.

When I look at what Eric has accomplished, I am truly inspired. eZWay is a true testament to what's possible when you let go of fear and let faith lead the way. I'm privileged to have gotten to know Eric, and honored to have worked with eZWay.

About Amy Thomson

Due to Amy's personal struggle with mental and physical health challenges, she spent over twenty-five years of her life studying self-improvement. She experimented with many different programs, in order to become confident, authentic, and empowered. As a result, she has created her own series of empowerment programs that will inspire others to make similar changes in their lives.

Amy Thomson is a:

- Homeschooling mother of children with special needs
- Productivity coach
- Bestselling author and multi-award winning artist/photographer
- TV Personality (*Where to Next*); Talk Show Host (*The Teresa & Amy Show*)
- Top 40 Under 40 Business Achievement Award Winner
- Coauthor of *Journeys to Success 2*, forwarded by Bob Proctor
- Think and Grow Rich Institute Science of Success Graduate
- Certified Life Coach with Canadian Federation of Coaches
- Landmark World Wide's Team Management and Leadership Program Alumni
- Founder of Affirming Arts™ and The Finisher's Club™
- Founder of Amy Thomson's 30 Days to Happiness Program

If you want to know more about Amy or Get Free Access to some of her programs and products, visit www.amythomson.ca

Email: Amy@AmyThomson.ca

Chapter 20

Holly Porter

I have always believed personal development was a huge part of business development, and if you want to do your best, you can't have one without the other.

Throughout the course of my life, I've created nine different startup companies. During that journey, I've learned several important lessons. The most important of those lessons is that money isn't everything! It sounds obvious, even simple, but it's true. You can prosper in so many other aspects of life: love, luck, hope, joy, and inner peace.

Most of my businesses have been service-based: spas, salons, a real estate brokerage, a fundraising company, daycare, preschool, and even a cement company. Each of these businesses has taught me how important it is to serve others. As a result, I began to study personality profiling.

If you work in sales, matching body language and energy is incredibly important. For example, if I'm speaking with an accountant, I know being factual and specific with my language will yield the most successful results. It will help this other person understand me better, and vice versa.

We are all different (obviously), and our brains are all wired differently. Everyone communicates in a slightly different fashion than everybody else. None of these different styles of communication are inherently wrong; in fact, it's perfect. It makes business (and life) much more interesting. It's up to us to learn the different ways people communicate, and adapt our business strategies to fit each particular situation. After all, if we're not learning and growing, then we aren't thriving. And if we're not thriving, then why are we even here?

Living a life of prosperity is a choice. It's up to you to decide if you truly want to live one. Remember: making a decision only takes one second. The rest of our time is usually spent figuring out why we made that decision, followed by a long period of time spent second-guessing that decision, which leads to procrastination, frustration, and many other negative emotions.

My life's journey has led me to the eZWay family. Eric and I have several mutual friends. I do not believe any of our common friends or acquaintances came into my life by accident. People enter our lives for a reason. Some people are there for years, others show up only for a moment, and it's up to us to make each person's moment count.

Eric has shown me nothing but kindness. I love the passion he has for what he does, I love his leadership skills, and I love his confidence. Eric has a generous heart, and he really wants to do well in the world. He wants to build people up. He wants us all to recognize our own amazing potential to change the world.

Sometimes it's difficult for us to see the greatness within ourselves, but Eric sees greatness in everyone. eZWay is the tool he provides to help them achieve that greatness. We all need cheerleaders in our lives, and Eric is a pretty darn good one.

I finally feel as though I'm settling into the kind of person I've always wanted to be. I'm creating a life I love, and I've attracted some pretty amazing people into that life. Eric is one of those people, and if he can help me bring out my greatness, I know he can do the same for you.

About Holly Porter

Holly Porter is an influencer, entrepreneur, and philanthropist. She is an international speaker who inspires business breakthroughs and personal transformations, helping audiences and clients everywhere formulate prosperous and sustainable businesses.

She has a gift for working with people. Holly is an active listener, an adept problem solver, and she puts her heart into her work. She knows what it takes to be successful, in business and in life, and she can help you achieve that same success for yourself.

Holly has created nine successful startup companies. She is the author of eleven books. Eight of those eleven books were #1 bestsellers. She has inspired over one hundred other women to reach new levels of personal and professional success.

When Holly isn't working with her clients, she can be found relaxing with her eight husband Scott Porter, their eight children, and eight grandchildren. She currently resides in St. George, Utah.

Chapter 21

Billy Moore

President ABC Youth Foundation

I met Eric through a mutual associate working with Dynamic Pay. This friend brought him to a meeting they were holding at a local coffee shop, and we hit it off right away. Eric and I both believe strongly in God and family. As a result of this introduction, we decided to start working on a website together.

Eric hosted an event in San Diego, CA, raising money for the ABC Youth Foundation. Over the years, we've developed a great friendship, and I've supported Eric in his many successful endeavors. In the end, we are both working to make a difference together for the ABC Youth Foundation.

I've served as president of the ABC Youth Foundation, an organization founded by my father, boxing legend Archie Moore. Our

mission is to empower San Diego's inner city youth to face life's challenges not with violence and cowardice, but with courage and dignity.

We provide an all-in-one after-school program in a safe, inviting
environment. We emphasize the importance of both academics and
athletics. We are equipped with a learning center and a gym. We offer
year-round programs, including a special enrichment course during
the summer break.

Our goal is to spread the ABC across the nation and put a perma-
nent stop to gang violence.

About Billy Moore

Mr. Bill Moore has been a highly touted member of the boxing community for over thirty years. He has worked with and trained some of
the best. Following the passing of his father Archie Moore, Billy has
served as president and CEO of the ABC Youth Foundation, a title he
has held for thirteen years.

Mr. Moore has touched the lives of hundreds of youth, and has
helped them become successful and productive members of society.
He has been a commentator and boxing color analyst for numerous
boxing broadcasts. He has been an active member of the San Diego
community for over thirty years.

Chapter 22

Dannella Burnett

Connections are the cornerstone for building a business. Today, we have more opportunities to connect than ever before, thanks to the Internet, social media, and mobile devices. Yet despite how connected everyone is with everyone else, we are witnessing an epidemic of loneliness, depression, and disconnection. Could this depression be prevented by fewer digital connections and more in-person connections? I think so.

In the professional realm, connections that leave us feeling empty, confused, or even taken advantage of, often will not result in successful business transactions. People choose to do business with those they trust, and that's no accident. That fact has become even more prevalent in this digital age we're living in.

Today, local and global information is readily available at a fingertip with just a few keystrokes. Sounds pretty convenient, but does this access to more information really giving us a feeling of connection, or is it just one more thing leaving us feeling empty? Maybe. But if these personal connections can't be found online, then where are they?

True connection is found in face-to-face interactions, in-person meetings, and even phone and video conferencing are good. But the best way to make new connections is at a live event. For me, every important business relationship has started, or become solidified, at a live event.

I chose my career path based on the realization that magical things happen when people come together. For example, I was nine years old when I was flipping through channels and found Julia Child on TV. I listened to her describe the food in her famous sing songy voice, I watched her serve her guests, and even as a nine-year-old, I could sense the connection between everyone at that table. I saw the connection between the people, the food, and the overall experience of it.

As I grew, I went on to become a chef, studying culinary arts at Johnson and Wales. For many years, I cooked for and managed restaurants in the Washington, D.C. area. Working with clients at special events, whether personal or professional, became my joy. And it still is to this day.

I eventually left D.C. and moved to Georgia, where I launched my catering company Oakwood Occasions. Although I loved working in the kitchen, I found myself becoming more interested in planning and executing a vision. I worked with speakers, authors, coaches, and national event hosts. My business was growing rapidly, and had expanded into three different and complementary businesses, all of which supported people and connections through live events.

Today, we serve clients local to Georgia through Oakwood Occasions and Lanier Tent and Event Rental. We also serve clients nationally, through Encore Elite Events. Frequently I get to witness life-changing moments and transformations that occur at live events, and sometimes I get to experience one of those transformative moments myself!

In fact, it was at one of these special events where I met Eric Zuley. We were both speakers and panelists at an event in California. The event was hosted by our mutual friend Allison Larson, and it was a day full of great presentations from speakers and entrepreneurs.

Throughout the second half of the day, Eric and I were seated next to one another on the panel. We exchanged pleasantries, and the more we chatted, it became apparent that we had a lot in common. We both gave our presentations, and afterwards we talked about the possibility of collaborating on a project. Eric introduced me to his father, James, and I of course fell in love with James' faith, his passion for helping veterans, and his pride in his son's achievements.

That day, I felt I had been given a glimpse into the vision behind eZWay. I got to experience its mission firsthand: to foster connections and to give more exposure to lesser-known business and nonprofits.

Over the past year, I've been welcomed into the eZWay family. I've been introduced to many talented and influential people, several of whom have shown up on the eZWay Wall of Fame. I'm excited to be a part of the eZWay event team. I love eZWay's mission to help businesses and nonprofits grow through collaboration, and I love how they've used the digital world to help people connect.

I've found the best way to grow is through face-to-face interactions, but eZWay does an excellent job promoting connectivity through social media. In this new digital world, they truly are the best of the best.

About Dannella Burnett

Dannella Burnett has been in the hospitality industry since she was sixteen years old. She has owned several businesses in Washington D.C. and Atlanta, GA. She's won numerous local, national, and international awards and is frequently featured in industry publications.

In 2008, she launched Oakwood Occasions to offer North Georgia clients hospitality and event services. Oakwood Occasions offers full service event planning, production, and a true partnership approach to create successful events guests will remember for years to come. In 2018, Oakwood was rebranded to Encore Elite Events in order to branch out and serve clients nationwide.

Oakwood's clients include national speakers, celebrities, networking associations, nonprofits, large corporations, etc. Dannella is also a live speaker, giving presentations on event strategies, female empowerment, and networking. She coaches speakers, event hosts, vendors, and sponsors. She is a creative force who truly believes that through collaboration, all parties can find a win-win solution to every problem.

Chapter 23

Robert Clancy

I met Eric in 2018. I was browsing social media when I stumbled upon one of his live broadcasts. Eric was interviewing a mutual business acquaintance, and I was immediately drawn in; I just had to keep watching this guy. Eric's energy, his enthusiasm, and his passion for making a difference was infectious.

I posted a comment on the broadcast. I said, and I quote: "Paying it forward is an expense we can all afford, and one humanity cannot live without."

This must have struck a chord with Eric. As soon as the broadcast ended, I received a private message from him, and we jumped on a call. I quickly learned this guy was the real deal. He told me how much he loves his father, both his biological father James, and his father in the sky (God). He shared how prayer helped him persevere when James was diagnosed with cancer. I immediately knew this was a guy I wanted to work with.

Eric's most amazing trait is his complete willingness to help someone get their message out. He champions messages that make a positive difference in the world. I feel honored to have had the opportunity to get to know him personally. He puts his heart into everything he does, whether that's promoting his brand, or promoting his clients. Eric will simply *get it done*. Give him an obstacle, place a barrier in his path, and he will either climb over that barrier or smash through it.

eZWay has been instrumental in helping me not only launch a successful show (*Mindset Reset*), but to also use that show to influence countless people. It premiered on Eric's eZWay Network and has featured notable guests like Dr. Joe Vitale, Kevin Sorbo, Dee Wallace, Arielle Ford, Marci Shim, and even Eric Zuley himself! eZWay has introduced me to influencers, bestselling authors, and producers.

Success breeds success - and that is exactly what eZWay brings to the table.

About Robert Clancy

Robert Clancy is a creative visionary, a #1 bestselling author, a spiritual teacher, and co-founder of Spiral Design, an award-winning creative firm specializing in graphic design and marketing. Spiral Design partners with a diverse base of clients, including Citi, Staples, The Home Depot, Activision, American Airlines, Geodynamics, Brooks Brothers, and The University at Albany, among many others. Clients range from Fortune 100s to nonprofits, with associations among the financial, legal, manufacturing, and educational industries.

At age nineteen, Robert experienced a divine spiritual encounter that altered his life in profound ways. In 2012, he created the Robert Clancy Guide to the Soul Facebook page, where he shares divinely inspired thoughts. The page is currently followed by nearly one million people worldwide.

He is a sought-after speaker, presenter, and guest. Robert is a regular contributor and weekly guest on Los Angeles KABC Radio's syndicated *Late Night Health Radio Show*. He is also the co-host and producer of the *Mindset Reset* television show (MindsetResetTV.com).

His latest book, *Soul Cyphers: Decoding a Life of Hope and Happiness*, quickly became a #1 international bestseller. Robert appeared on the 2018-19 season Emmy® Award winning *Dr. Nandi Show*. His appearance was watched by over three hundred million people on several major cable and satellite networks, including Discovery and ABC.

Awards and Honors

- Gold Worldwide ADDY® Advertising Award
- The Business Review "40 under 40" Award
- Junior Achievement Ambassador Award
- Hugh O'Brian Youth Leadership Outstanding National Seminar Chairperson
- NYS Junior Chamber of Commerce Governor Award
- NYS Small Business Development Center 'Entrepreneur of the Year'
- Capital Region Chamber "Van Rensselaer Award" for community service
- 5th Degree Master Black Belt Martial Arts Instructor

Chapter 24

Kate Linder

I was born on November 2, 1947. After graduating high school, I moved to San Francisco, where I attended San Francisco State University, majoring in drama. I participated in many local stock and repertory theatres in the Bay area.

After earning my degree in Theatre Arts, I stayed in San Francisco, dividing my time between the stage and exotic locales around the world. What spare time I had was spent working in the University's activities office where I met my future husband, Dr. Ronald Linder, who was then a professor at the school. After marrying him, we relocated to Los Angeles, where I broke into the TV scene, earning guest-starring roles in several sitcoms and dramas.

In April 1982, I was cast on *The Young and the Restless*. It was only supposed to be a small role, but instead, I remained a main cast member for over thirty years. On April 10, 2008, I received a star on the

Hollywood Walk of Fame. I was previously elected to two terms as the Governor of Daytime Programming Peer Group for the Academy of Television Arts and Sciences (the folks who put on the Emmy Awards), and I'm a longtime board member for SAG-AFTRA.

On the silver screen, I've had the pleasure of starring in *Hysteria* (2012), *Erased* (2013), *Miss Meadows* (2014), *Better Off Single* (2016), *Mother's Day* (2016), *Voice from The Stone* (2017), *The Charnel House* (2017), *Dead Love* (2018) and I'm a lead in Charlie Matthau's *Book of Leah* (2019) and *Loaners* (2019).

I met Eric years ago, when Gregory J. Martin introduced me to him on the set of *The Bay*. I admire his tenacity. He reminds me of myself in that he never gives up. If the answer is no, he keeps going until he gets a yes. I am honored to be part of Eric's journey, and I'm looking forward to many more incredible experiences with the eZWay family.

About Kate Linder

Kate Linder is the celebrity spokesperson for the ALS Association, the preeminent leader in the fight against Lou Gehrig's Disease. She sits on the board of SAG-AFTRA, and can be found most holidays serving food to the hungry and homeless at the Los Angeles Mission.

On April 10, 2008, Kate received a star on the Hollywood Walk of Fame, and for the past thirty-seven years, she has worked both as a daytime television actress and a United Airlines flight attendant.

She is active with the USO, and visits troops in the US, in Afghanistan, Pakistan, Korea and Guantanamo Bay. In late 2005, Kate was elected Governor of the Daytime Programming Peer Group of the Academy of Television Arts and Sciences. In 2007, she was reelected for a second two-year stint.

Despite some of the hardships Kate has endured, she remains an eternal optimist and tireless worker for many charities. She was named celebrity spokesperson for The ALS Association in early 2005. Her late brother-in-law was diagnosed with Lou Gehrig's Disease in December 2004, and she has traveled to Washington, D.C. each May to lobby for more funds to fight the disease. In 2006, Kate won the organization's All-Star Award for her passionate service to the cause and won their Packman Award in 2007, as well as the One Starry Night Award in 2016.

Today, Kate travels around the country to participate in ALS (Lou Gehrig's Disease) Association fundraisers and encourages other volunteers to lead fundraising dinners for local chapters. She is active with many AIDS charities and the Los Angeles Mission. In addition, Kate also hosts three annual charity teas with a rotating group of her cast mates - one for Canucks for Kids every July in Vancouver, and another two in Toronto and Calgary for March of Dimes Canada's Conductive Education® program (an organization that helps children and adults with neuro-motor disabilities).

Chapter 25

Fred Smith

I met Eric Zuley in 2006, at a red carpet event in Beverly Hills. It was a magazine launch, and I was the DJ; he was the rapper. At the time, Eric was also hosting his own channel, "What U Need TV."

Together, we redefined the standard of how a team should work in Hollywood. We dressed up and attended hard to access events in prestigious venues. Basically, we were the unicorns in a room full of mainstream entertainment outlets.

We've helped each other a lot through the years. We've worked through several pivots the company has made, and eZWay has reminded me that there are good people doing great things out there. Those people simply need a platform, and eZWay created one.

My personal story is too long to tell. What I can say is that I'm grateful and humbled to work with Eric, and to have partnered with eZWay.

About Fred Smith:

Leadyourpower.info
Businessscaling.com
https://www.juggernaut.marketing/

Chapter 26

Jonny (Vegas) Namer

I was first introduced to Eric Zuley and his Father James Zuley in 2011, at a party at my father's house in Encino, California. We soon discovered we had a lot of things in common, and we've been friends ever since.

My life revolves around my lacrosse career. I have played lacrosse since 2001, when I was 14. Since then, I've built several successful brands/companies under the Jonny Vegas Entertainment Umbrella. I am a successful podcast host, writer, journalist, photographer, videographer, emcee, Semi-Pro Lacrosse Team Co-Owner/Co-General Manager, graphic designer, and a social media influencer.

Eric has interviewed me on his shows. Several times, as a matter of fact. He introduced me to the Lingerie Basketball League owner and players, and has invited me to several events over the years. A few years back, Eric's father James even filmed one of my lacrosse games.

About Jonny "Vegas" Namer

Jonny Vegas is the founder and president of Jonny Vegas Inc. He began in California, building a name and reputation for himself within the lacrosse community. His passion for lacrosse and his knowledge of football, basketball, hockey, baseball, boxing, mixed martial arts, wrestling, and soccer have propelled him into his own niche in the entertainment industry.

His accomplishments include:

- South Bay Lacrosse Club in the SCLA since 2016
- Total Lacrosse ASTROS in Sin City Box Classic (SCBC)
- Shootout for Soldiers Event, Orange County, CA
- Culver City's Finest in the ULAX Los Angeles league
- Navy Gold in the Jam by the Sea Tournament, San Diego, CA
- Total Lacrosse Universe in Hawaii Lacrosse Invitational, Honolulu, HI
- Midlife Creases in the Tribz Lacrosse California Showcase, Irvine, CA
- Hammerheads in the ULAX Los Angeles League
- Istanbul Sultans in the Ales Hrebesky Memorial Box Lacrosse Tournament in Prague, Czech Republic
- Salt Shakerz in the Jam by The Sea Tournament in San Diego, CA
- Salt Shakerz in the Las Vegas Lacrosse Showcase 2013
- Turkey's National Lacrosse Team, Turkey in Ashkelon, Israel
- Total lacrosse Vegas in the SB Brawl in Santa Barbara, CA
- Salt Shakerz in the Lake Tahoe Lacrosse Tournament in Lake Tahoe NV

- Ventura County Bombers, NKA Los Angeles Bombers in the West Coast Lacrosse Spring Leave in Camarillo, CA
- Devils Box Lacrosse Team in the West Coast Lacrosse Summer Leave, Camarillo, CA
- Team AWESOME, in the Vail Lacrosse Shootout, Vail, CO
- Team LAX, NKA Venice Lacrosse Club, in the SCLA
- Beverly Hills Bucks in the SCLA
- Warriors Box Lacrosse Team in the West Coast Lacrosse team in El Segundo, CA
- began in the Conejo Middle School Goonies in the Conejo Valley Lacrosse League (CVLL) continuing to play at Westlake High school, graduating in 2006

Chapter 27

Theresa Ashby

I am a strategist. I know, understand, and study strategy and what it means to businesses. I've been recognized as a savvy, provocative, and genuine individual, and within my circle of clients and business partners, I am highly respected.

I absolutely love working dedicated business leaders. I want founders, entrepreneurs, executives, and investors to call on me when they need consulting. I know what it takes to run an organization, I know all the challenges and pressures that come with the job, and I want to collaborate with business owners. If they need help, I provide it, and if they want to become successful, I can teach them how. If I can help someone build their empire (and have a great team surrounding them), then I am all-in.

It took me a little while to realize that dream, though. In 2014, I was working for a billion-dollar organization, I was bringing in a six-figure income, with full insurance coverage and a retirement plan. I ran nine different departments, and I led hundreds of people (while also managing a $50 million budget). On paper, it would appear as if I had it all, and perhaps I did, but the truth was, I felt deeply unsatisfied with that life.

I felt as though I wasn't really contributing enough. I knew I had talents, I knew I had drive, and I wanted to use my talents for a greater purpose. I was completely checked out from my career at that point. During business meetings, I would drift off into daydreams. *What could I do, if I were someplace else?* I liked the idea of leaving and starting my own consulting business, where I would be free to coach more people and help more businesses.

I knew I needed to do something greater than what I was doing at that point: sitting in this glass cage, serving only a small population of people. There was more to my professional life than working for this company, so I left.

Several months later, I reconnected with Eric. We had met previously (we once shared a stage at one of his events), but I wanted to get to know him on a deeper level. I was intrigued by his dedication, generosity, and his passion for giving to nonprofit organizations.

So we met at a coffee shop, and we chatted nonstop. I don't think there was a single moment of silence throughout our entire meeting. He told me about his newest project, which was a nonprofit organization he was raising money for.

If you know Eric, then you know the energy he brings into every conversation. We went live on social media, and he interviewed me, introducing me to all of his friends and colleagues. We hadn't even made a formal business deal; nothing was set in stone yet, but that didn't matter to Eric. He was energetic, enthusiastic, and very excited to share his knowledge with me.

I attended more of his fundraisers, I watched him work, and I knew this guy was efficient. I knew he knew what he was doing, and I could see he knew exactly how to get a job done. I began realizing Eric could help make my dream come true, and that dream was to become an influencer.

I needed help from an expert, and Eric had exactly the kind of expertise I was looking for. I had very few connections, and I had no idea how to build my business around a social media platform. I was an influencer in search of a proper outlet.

The first thing Eric did was create a fast-track plan suited to the specific needs of my business. He introduced me to many other influencers. He and I collaborated on remodeling my website. He invited me to exclusive events. He set me up with new capture and texting software to help build my funnel.

Today, my business has changed in more ways than I could have ever imagined. Eric and his team have been instrumental in hat change. Eric always tells me: "I am here to let you do what you do, let others know what you do, how you can be of service to them." Every time I get a call from him (and that's quite often), he tells me about another opportunity he has secured for me.

Eric and I share many things in common, including a strong work ethic. When I work with my clients, I work at a very fast pace, providing excellent services catered to each client's specific needs. This is how Eric works, too—he never stops thinking about what's coming next.

About Dr. Theresa Ashby

Dr. Theresa Ashby is a national business and success consultant, an advisor, speaker, and author. She is passionate about driving businesses forward, and her ability to unite teams around one common vision has been paramount to her success.

Her background includes thirty years of experience in a variety of leadership roles, managing a $50 million budget, overseeing $1.7 billion of capital improvement, running hundreds of teams at once, and implementing operational strategies. She served as vice president of operations for a leading healthcare organization, and vice president of the National Association of Women Business Owners-California.

She is the author of *Better Implementation NOW! Eight Ways Great Strategies Fail & How to Fix Them.* She is also the CEO of Strategic Implementation Solutions, and assistant professor at Loma Linda University.

Chapter 28

Denise Millett-Burkhardt

I met Eric Zuley in November 2017, through a dear friend Freddy K (of Freddy K Media Promotions). By February 2018, Eric was my CMO, with 30 potential shows valued at 10 million dollars per contract, equaling $300 million. Eric has brought in several networks and has grown my company substantially. He also was the reason that I received two very special awards, of which I have humbly accepted. These were The City of Los Angeles Certificate of Recognition Producer's Award for heartfelt support of Multicultural International Motion Picture Association making Los Angeles a better place to live and work; and The Certificate of Special Congressional Recognition of outstanding and invaluable service to the community. These would not have been possible without my association with Eric Zuley.

That same year, we started eZWay TV Network with the following additions:

-May: Regalia TV Network, with investor Michael Davis

-End of May/June: Guiding Star with investor Robert Clancey, Glory Media with Pastor Dr. Chapman and Dr. Hardwick, involving 52,000 churches across the United States.

-July: Youth Success Network, with Andrew Blume and Lisa Winston (Dr. Joe Vatalis "The Secret Knock") and Advantage TV with Jeffrey Stansfield, (Designer and builder of 250 TV Stations)

-December: The High Performance Success Network with Suzette Bailey and Linda Cain of Creative Supernova, and William Meers.

Two of these networks, Guiding Star and Youth Success Network, are charity networks. Eric is continually involved with charities, ranging from charities that fight to end homelessness among veterans, to organizations that help get thousands of children adopted through foster care programs. He also works with the American Cancer Society.

Eric and I have worked together with many people who are doing great things. Some of these include: Dr. Olympia Gellini of the United Nations Peace Ambassador, Frank Shankwitz of Make a Wish Foundation, Billie Moore (Archie Moore Sons) ABC Foundation, Bobbi DePorter and Stedman Graham Jr. of CAYS Foundation & Youth Success Network, Lori Director of VANC (Veterans Association of North County) and the American Cancer Society, Alyssa Milano with Women's Veterans Groups, and Xavier Mitchell, owner of OKTV for Autism Awareness, and James Dentley of JD3 TV Network.

Eric does not discriminate against color, creed, or religion, and will give a helping hand to anyone in need. For the past year and a half, we have given away $300,000 a week for charity, air time, and donation commercials. Sometimes that amount has been doubled. He is selfless, exemplary and noticed by so many.

Eric has brought extensive media exposure across several different platforms, groups, text ads, and commercials. I have been to so many wonderful events and have met so many creative and compassionate entrepreneurs. Thanks to Eric, my life and my business have been enriched.

We are now working on a project called Vetterlands. (Vetterlands.com and vetterlands.org) Sandrena Schumacher, Alecsandre Schumacher, Eric Zuley and myself plan to house over 10,000 homeless veterans in Imperial County, California. We will provide housing, a wellness center, and a hotel, all working towards transitioning these veterans back into society. There will also be an airport and helicopter pad, a reservoir, RV park, and 20 grow houses we will extend to the VA hospitals, schools, and homeless. Each of these houses will feed 100,000 people per year.

With the assistance of Pattie Sadler and Scott Nugent, we have come very far in giving back to the veterans who gave everything for us. If you would like to participate in the Vetterlands project, please contact us. It is our belief that those who defended the streets should not be sleeping on them.

Chapter 29

Brian Smith, "Mr. UGG"

Seven years ago, Eric and I met at the Los Angeles Convention Center at one of his events. In him, I saw a strong work ethic, drive, determination, and tenacity. I immediately gave him my business card. We continued to see each other at many other events, we shared a few stages together, and we became very good friends.

About Brian Smith

At 29, Brian decided that a life in Public Accounting was not for him. He quit his job and moved out to California, looking for a new business idea, and to surf the legendary breaks. He soon noticed that there were no sheepskin boots in California, so he and a friend brought six pairs from Australia to test. After that, "UGG" was born, and over the next seventeen years, Brian built it into a national brand, solidifying himself as a business expert.

Pretty soon, the business grew too large for Brian to finance, so he sold it to Deckers Outdoor Corporation. The new team built upon the "casual comfort" theme, and through style development, merchandising, and great marketing, established UGG as an international fashion brand. Over the last five years, sales have exceeded one billion dollars.

In 2000, Brian founded Prefast, a company that provided pre-cast concrete walls for California schools. He sold this business, and the company continues to build California schools to this day. In 2003, he patented a new precast wall panel that incorporates lightweight concrete and steel studs. Over one hundred of these steel and concrete structures were built before the economic recession in 2008.

Today, Brian is one of the most sought-after speakers and business leaders in the country. His inspirational talks and media appearances are widely attended by business people of all ages. Brian has been designated by *Footwear News* as one of the most influential people in footwear during the past century.

http://briansmithspeaker.com/about/

Chapter 30

Pattie Godfrey~Sadler, Founder/CEO of New Life Clarity Publishing

I met Eric three years ago at an event organized by another influencer. Eric was there, interviewing and spotlighting some of the guests. I had the opportunity so speak to him one-on-one, and I told him I wanted to get back to work on my old talk show (I had taken a hiatus to care for my elderly parents). Eric was genuinely interested in what I had to say, and that very day, he interviewed me live.

After the interview, I had so many new messages and friend requests that I was beside myself. Already I was gaining momentum and amassing a large following, and we hadn't even been working together very long. Over the months that followed, Eric became my biggest supporter, and he helped me spread my message to so many people. From day one, he has included me in everything and anything he thinks will help me.

I've been watching Eric, and have been simply amazed by his dedication to his eZWay family members. He created a space for his clients, he takes everyone's efforts to heart, and he's full of gratitude. His love for God and his love for his father, James Zuley, have been inspiring. Eric has always been loyal and trustworthy. I'm so grateful to call this young man a friend, and I'm positively honored to have been welcomed into the eZWay family.

I have a passion for the human experience, I love to write, and my cause is to help women all over the globe realize their potential. I have a skill for motivating other people and making them smile. All these qualities have built a solid foundation for me to be of service to others. That's where my joy lies: serving others. My mission is to motivate and inspire others, in the hopes that those people will go out into the world and motivate or inspire more people, thus creating an endless cycle of positivity.

Inspiring others is actually quite simple. You have talents, right? Everyone does. Make use of them. Offer your service whenever and wherever you are able. In doing so, you are manifesting more joy in the world. You *can* make a difference. You *can* change lives. By sharing your talents, you'll come to realize how valuable you really are.

Achieve clarity in all aspects of your life. Consider your health, your spirituality, personal development, personal relationships, and your financial/career development. Get personal coaching, if you need it. use journaling or freewriting to express your thoughts, feelings, and desires. Create a plan of action. Organize your life, and things will start falling into place.

Meditate daily. Your mind believes what it's told, so avoid giving it negative reinforcement. Replace those negative thoughts with positive ones. We all struggle to fight those overwhelming negative thoughts, and it's essential to recognize that negativity as the lie that it is. Focus on the positive, rather than dwell on the negative, and you will begin to find inspiration everywhere you look.

If you are good at something, make it yours and brand it! Create business cards. For example, if you're starting a consulting business, your cards should state what your specialty is. Other people should be able to clearly recognize what you can offer them. Motivate others to get involved with your plan. Believe in yourself, and take on the challenge. You are the only one who can take on this creative effort. It won't always be easy, and it won't always be fun, but it's worth it in the long run.

Believe in yourself. Never give up, no matter how hard the journey gets. Share your ideas, network with others, and choose your associates wisely. Make sure their goals and passions align with yours, and you might be surprised at what you can create together. Your talents and abilities are worth seeing through to the end. If you put your heart into it, there's no telling what sorts of amazing contributions you'll give to the world.

Remember: money should not be the motivating factor for doing what you do. Money may come as a result, but following your dreams should be the primary goal. Money's just a bonus. It allows us to contribute to society, and to provide our families a better quality of life.

Think big. Be grandiose. Playing small serves no one, least of all ourselves. We were all designed to make a difference in this world. So embrace it! There's no reason to doubt your natural abilities. Be a fierce entrepreneurial warrior. Become your own miracle, and change the world!

About Pattie Godfrey~Sadler

World-class speaker and consultant, Pattie Godfrey-Sadler has a passion for the human story. She believes every person has the potential to influence and inspire the world. Pattie Sadler is the founder of the New Life Clarity Project, a nonprofit organization that helps people create real change in their lives. The NLCP provides tools for women to overcome domestic abuse, addiction, and other traumas.

Pattie is also the founder/CEO of New Life Clarity Publishing, creating a space for men and women alike to share their stories with the world. NLCP gives authors the necessary tools to sell their books internationally.

Pattie is also a talk show host and PR director in the SOaR Foundation. She lives life with passion, and has a talent for inspiring others to figure out the big WHY in their lives. She also acts as a counselor, trainer, and first responder for PTSD patients.

In the professional world, she has assisted business owners, sales teams, entrepreneurs, and authors in creating their ideal businesses. Pattie believes "we are all divinely created for greatness," and helps others manifest their visions, making the dreams in their heads become a reality.

Chapter 31

Penny Foskaris

Wellness Leader & Consultant

I grew up in a family of restaurateurs, and thus, proper nutrition was a huge part of my daily life. I began studying nutrition long before I received my formal education in the field. Due to the obesity epidemic and the prevalence of type 2 diabetes in America, serving on the Community Leadership Board with the American Diabetes Association was incredibly important to me.

I joined the American Academy of Anti-Aging Medicine. I recently created Foskaris Wellness; our flagship location is in Anaheim Hills, CA. Along with our in-office services, Foskaris Wellness offers a wide variety of digital services including nutritional genetic testing, customized meal plans, as well as several different coaching programs. Foskaris Wellness utilizes a holistic approach combined with state-of-the-art technology, in order to achieve the fastest, safest, and least invasive fat loss results for our clients.

I briefly met Eric at a couple networking events in 2019. In June, I'd just come home from a 14-hour day at the office. I opened Facebook, only to see Eric had just started a live video, so I said hello. After the video, Eric and I discussed business. I liked what eZWay had to offer, so we discussed the possibility of working together.

Working with eZWay has given me exposure to amazing people I wouldn't have been able to meet. Eric introduced me to so many of my valuable clients. In addition to giving my brand exposure, he also taught me five basic steps to starting a new and successful business:

1. Research your market. Find out if there is truly a need for your type of business.
2. Find a great marketing specialist. Make sure they understand your business.
3. Have a good team supporting you. You can't do everything yourself. You could get burnt out, or possibly even quit.
4. Don't be afraid to ask for help. You might find that one of your friends/family has the proper skills to help with the task at hand.
5. The most important tip of all: Remember to take some time to care for yourself. Get enough sleep and eat a proper diet.

About Penny Foskaris

Find out more about Penny and her team at www. FoskarisWellness.com

Chapter 32

John Highland

I've seen Eric at numerous events. I've watched this man put others before himself. I reached out to him, hoping he would join one of our mastermind groups. He did, and he ended up not only filling the room with quality people, but he also streamed the event live to 1500 online viewers. Impressed, I ended up bringing eZWay in as a premier partner to Speaking Empire.

About John Highland

John is a motivational speaker, business coach, speaker, trainer. He is a husband of 29 years, and the father of two awesome children. He graduated with a degree in financing from Liberty University, and immediately started a telecommunications company in 1988. Over time, his company expanded to over 400 employees and installed over 12,000 miles of fiber optic cables in the U.S. If you make a phone call or use the internet, there's a good chance you are using one of the lines his company installed.

In 2003, his major clients, MCI WorldCom and Adelphia Business Solutions, went bankrupt, owing John and his company over $7 million. He sold his franchised restaurants and mortgaged his house, just to pay his payroll. He took his business experience and his construction company and moved into a lucrative housing business. He built or renovated over 200 homes and buildings. He has met every living HUD (Housing and Urban Development) Secretary since Jack Kemp. The largest house he built was a 20,000 square foot mansion in Columbus, Ohio. Over the last ten years, John has sold over 2,000 properties.

John started speaking internationally in 2003. He has spoken in Iceland, Israel, Japan, Canada, the Philippines, Hong Kong, Taiwan, Macau, Mexico, and all over the United States. From the stage, he has sold approximately $20 million in educational and motivational courses.

He now promotes other speakers and their products, and he speaks on some of the largest seminar stages in the world, including Learning Annex, Get Motivated, and many others. He serves as a board member of a charity that helped over 150 young men and women get Division 1 basketball and volleyball scholarships. Some well-known alumni from that charity include Yao Ming, (Houston Rockets), Lorenzo Romar, (University of Arizona, Assistant Head Coach), and recently Marvin Bagley (Duke) and Cody Riley, UCLA).

Chapter 33

Sophia Alvarez

At the tender age of two, I, and my six-month-old sister, were abandoned by our mother and rescued by our grandparents. To this day, I don't know or understand why she left. When my grandparents found us, I was trying to bottle-feed my baby sister. Our neighbor heard us and contacted them, and for the rest of our childhoods, we lived with my grandparents.

We had a new home, but it wasn't a stable home. My grandfather was an abusive alcoholic who often assaulted my grandmother. As I grew older, I slowly started taking on the role of protector over my grandmother and younger sister. I would stay awake late at night to make sure Grandpa didn't beat up Grandma. If I did end up falling asleep, the police would often show up to put a stop to the fight that would inevitably break out.

Grandpa once fired a gun at the ceiling. Another time he drove his station wagon into the house. On a separate occasion, he tried hanging himself with telephone wire in the front doorway. It was a crazy environment for my sister and I to grow up in. When Grandpa wasn't drinking, he was a totally different person. He was warm, caring, and affectionate. He was almost unrecognizable from the alcoholic battering my grandmother. It wasn't a very safe living environment, but at that point in my life, I was used to living in unsafe environments.

I spent a lot of my early childhood in the streets of La Puente, Bassett, and El Monte. These were areas ravaged by gang activity. On our particular street stood something we called "The Dead End Wall." If a gang member was killed in the area, their name was written on that wall.

The only safety net I had was a Spanish church across the street. I attended Bible school every summer. As all that gang activity closed in on us, I found Christ. I learned language does not matter, so long as you've got the spirit. Jesus passes through all language barriers.

When I was sixteen, I met my husband-to-be, and at seventeen, we were married. My grandmother signed the papers. Throughout our marriage, we had three children: one son and two daughters.

I later became involved in ministry, as I began experiencing uplifting and life-changing experiences during the course of my life. My friend Kara Madden and I started our own ministry, "Total Surrender Evangelistic Team Ministries." Soon after, I met a man named Ryan Torres, the owner/founder of *Avenue Entertainment Magazine*. Ryan would later become part of the ministry, and it was through him that I met Eric Zuley.

I worked with Ryan's magazine for a short period, helping with casting, and through him, I entered the entertainment business. A few short years later, I approached Eric and asked how I could get involved with his broadcasting platform.

He took me under his wing, and we started working the red carpets. I had the pleasure of watching his dreams come to full fruition.

I have never seen anyone work as hard as this amazing young man does. I've worked in all areas of eZWay, and I've seen the endless calls, I watched people using him, abusing his talents, but he never let that stop him. He always continued pushing forward. I do it the eZWay.

Let me share some of the life lessons I've learned, over the course of working with this truly incredible man:

1. Never let anyone steal your dream. Only you can paint your vision, and it belongs to you.
2. Be yourself! Don't change for anyone.
3. Never give up!
4. Pray. Talk with Jesus. He will never lead you astray.
5. Not everyone will believe in you. Sometimes you have to walk your path alone.
6. The Internet is full of courses and materials that can help you further your knowledge. Use this precious resource!
7. Lastly, YOU HAVE TO WORK! You may procrastinate, you may doubt your skills, you may fail, and that's alright; we all fail, but nothing worthwhile comes without hard work.

Chapter 34

Brenton Tyler Hoffmann

At the age of 7, I was diagnosed with severe ADHD, as well as a learning disability. I was held back in kindergarten twice, and was later placed in special education classes for the rest of my scholastic life.

I endured thirteen long years of horrific child abuse. I was bullied and beaten up by gangs, I've had guns put in my face, I've even been chased with knives by one of my stepdads. I survived thirty years of debilitating depression and anxiety.

On Thanksgiving Day 1998, I was involved in an automobile accident, shattering my vertebrae and paralyzing myself from the neck down. Somehow, miraculously, I walked away twelve hours later, after the doctors repeatedly told me I would never walk again, and I did it without any surgery or physical therapy.

Throughout my life, many close friends have died. I've lost the love of my life twice, I've lost countless jobs, I lost my home of fourteen years, and resorted to living in my car for nearly five hundred days.

Even though everything looked hopeless, nothing could stop me from giving up on my dream.

During this homeless period, I decided it was time to start working on my heart and mind. I did just that, and I started feeding other homeless people, sharing my meals with them, even though sometimes I barely had enough to feed myself. I got to know these people. I listened to their stories.

This was a huge turning point for me. It was then that I realized there had to be more to this life than suffering. Through my relentless perseverance, persistence, and patience, I kept going, I kept living even though life did not look hopeful. Not even death could stop me, and eventually, I turned my life around. I moved into a new home, I raised my credit score, I met an amazing success coach, and I learned how to identify, ignore, and defeat negative, disempowering beliefs.

Shortly after working with my coach, I reconnected with my mother and brother, who I'd fallen out with. I met Eric Zuley. I learned from him and JT Foxx about the power of branding, and I used their teachings to help build and brand my own coaching company.

Eric has helped me many times over the years, both in my personal and professional life. He gave me a platform when no one else would. He introduced me to many successful people in the entertainment industry. He's helped with my PR. Thanks to Eric, I've been featured in publications such as *Associated Press*, and celebrity websites like Wire Image.

I've been featured on *Actors Reporter*, an entertainment website with over three million subscribers. I've done radio interviews on *LA Talk Radio* and eZWayBroadcasting. Over the last ten years, Eric has introduced me to several great people, many of whom I'm still friends with today. His social media knowledge has helped me increase audience engagement on virtually every social media platform.

Now, my life purpose is to inspire as many people as humanly possible. I want to encourage them to keep going, no matter what. I want to motivate others to find their true purpose, help other people, and create a ripple effect that will continue to live on long after I'm gone.

I am immensely grateful for what Eric has done for me. For the last ten years, I have been running my life (and my business) the eZWay.

If you are done struggling and want more success in all areas of life, reach out to me for a one-on-one Discovery Session.

facebook.com/harmonikconsulting

About Brenton Hoffmann

Brenton Hoffmann is an inspirational coach, philosopher, and visionary. He is a student of Jim Rohn, Les Brown, Brian Tracy, Tony Robbins, Tim Zimmerman of SM3 Success, and JT Foxx (The Worlds #1 Wealth Coach). He is highly trained in the area of personal development, social dynamics, NLP, and human psychology. Brenton is a communicator, empath, and problem solver.

He has known Eric Zuley since 2010, when he served as Eric's executive networking assistant and co-host of WTV Networks. Brenton has inspired many people in many fields, including teachers, CEOs, and entrepreneurs. He helped coach, train, advise, and inspire clients to attain their goals, from winning sought-after movie roles to winning Toastmasters Top Speaker Awards, overcoming their fears, running their first marathon, getting their next belt in martial arts, and even getting invited to the UN.

Brenton was an award-winning skateboarder, martial artist, gymnast, professional aggressive-inline-skater, guitarist/pianist, celebrity hip-hop recording artist, magician/illusionist, TV co-host, actor, sales expert, master energy healer, and professional networking expert.

He has been featured in celebrity media publications such as *The Examiner, eZWay, Actors Reporter, LA Talk Radio*, WIRE/Getty

Images, & *The Associated Press*, as well as television networks like ABC, CBS USA NBC, FOX, & The CW.

He was inducted into the eZWay Hall of Fame, along with celebrities like Christopher Lloyd (*Back to The Future*) Bill Duke, plus many more. Brenton was recently nominated for the 2019 Resilience Award.

Chapter 35

Jeffrey Stansfield

I met Eric at an event we both happened to be speaking at. Eric's girlfriend actually introduced us. Once I got to know him and what he did, I was impressed by his social media reach and TV distribution. Eric connected me with more clients and regularly helped me book speaking gigs. It was the perfect match, honestly. We had the equipment, and he had the reach.

My strategy for Success

1) Shut up and listen to others.
2) Invest in yourself and always keep learning.
3) Give back to others.
4) Always be truthful
5) Promote others before yourself. You will find if you lift up others, they will lift you even higher.

About Jeffrey Stansfield

Jeffrey Stansfield is the president and CEO of Advantage Video Systems, a leading technology provider to the broadcast, motion picture, television and motion graphics industries. Stansfield launched AVS in 2001, and has steadily built its clientele by focusing on one customer at a time. His slogan, "How can we make your day perfect?" drives him and his team to empower clients with the latest information and technology solutions. His company's work encompasses workflow consultation, design, installation, and integration.

Stansfield has served as a general board member, treasurer, and secretary of SMPTE (Society of Motion Picture and Television Engineers). He supports several industry organizations including the Creative Pro User Group Network, the Digital Cinema Society, the Hollywood Post Alliance, the Society of Television Engineers, and the National Association of Broadcasters. He has over 34 years of experience in the business, including the construction of broadcast facilities and providing technology services for production/post-production facilities.

Stansfield is a certified editor in Final Cut, Avid and Adobe Premiere, and a beta tester for Adobe After Effects and Premiere. He holds certifications in cabling systems, including fiber, and offers his unique expertise in camerawork, lighting, shared storage, and asset management solutions.

Chapter 36

Ronald Couming

I met Eric Zuley via social media. Throughout our working relationship, Eric has helped me increase my following. He has given me access to countless influencers. He and I have worked as partners in several capacities, including networking and television.

My Success strategy is as follows:

1. Focus on ROR not ROI, (ROR) Return on Relationships, (ROI) Return on Investment. Build quality relationships, and never focus on one-off sales.
2. Put yourself in the room with people playing 3-5 times higher than the level you are.
3. Seek counsel, not advice. Counsel comes from someone who has been there and done that; advice is simply an opinion.

4. Surround yourself with only OQP (Only Quality People). Stay away from negative people; they have a problem for every solution.

5. Live on the 2 CC track system. When considering an opportunity, event, business relationship, etc., apply the two CC's (Contribute or Contaminate). Does it contribute to or contaminate my life, mission, or goals?

For 8 easy tips to success go to:
https://rcsonlinesolutions.com/seo-tips/

About Ronald Couming

Ronald Couming is an Internet Marketing and SEO Expert. He's the founder and CEO of RCS Online Solutions, LLC. He is an internationally recognized speaker, published author, radio show host, and successful entrepreneur. Ronald's passion is helping business owners "achieve even greater success" by creating scalable and sustainable business models.

He is an Internet marketing expert, and has lent his expertise to nearly 100,000 entrepreneurs and small businesses across the country. He has spoken on stages all over the world, via in-person events and webinars. He has a wide variety of expertise, including Internet marketing, business solutions, technology, self-development, leadership, team building, and entrepreneurship. He has created an innovative approach to helping businesses and business owners achieve extraordinary and sustainable success.

Chapter 37

Leisa Reid

Eric and I met at a party hosted by TR Garland. Eric and I connected right away, and we kept in touch. We decided to collaborate on a project at some point in the future.

eZWay has helped me realize the weight of the impact I'd like to make in the world. Eric thinks big and moves fast! He sees opportunity where every-

one else sees only failure. He helped me discover innovative new ways to take what I'm doing to the next level.

****

After booking a total of 400 speaking engagements, the most frequent question I'm asked is: "How can I get more speaking gigs?" The underlying question is: "How can I, as a speaker, attract more clients?"

The first thing I tell these up-and-coming speakers is to collaborate with others. Working with other people is key. I often ask my clients/business partners how I can best support them. I show them I'm looking out for their needs, and that makes a significant contribution to my success. People want to work with someone who cares about their success.

Remember those 400 speaking engagements I mentioned? 30% of those came from collaborations with others. In my mastermind, The Speaker Collab Experience, I mentor speakers on utilizing collaboration in order to get and *stay* booked.

The second piece of advice I give new and/or struggling speakers is to be themselves, but also have a plan. Often, people say to "be authentic" or "transparent." While it *is* important to demonstrate your unique qualities to attract clients, it is also important to have a strategy in place, so that what you're sharing aligns with your vision and purpose. When I mentor speakers, I try to highlight their true message, and I help them devise a strategy to get the best possible results.

My third piece of advice is to be curious. I am truly interested in connecting with people. Genuine curiosity has helped me book those 400+ speaking engagements. It all starts with genuine interest that can often lead to a deep connection.

As a speaker, it's important to ask lots of questions throughout the booking process:

"How can I best serve your audience?"

"Would it be okay if I told them how they can continue working with me?"

"When you say it's okay to sell, can you tell me more so that I'm in alignment with your group?"

By asking these types of questions, you can eliminate the assumptions you've made that may or may not be true. I'm able to share scripts and strategies with my speaking clients, in the hope that they'll learn to ask questions in a way that isn't pushy or creepy.

Also, consistency is key. After running the OC Speakers Network (www.ocSpeakersNetwork.com) monthly since 2013, one of my keys to success had been remaining consistent. Those meetings are on the first Tuesday of every month at the same time and in the same venue. It's much easier to keep your momentum going when you're consistent.

It doesn't hurt to give away some sort of free gift at the end of your presentation (or at the end of your chapter in a book). Here's a perfect demonstration of how to provide extra value for your audience. This is an actual free gift from me to you:

Visit www.GetSpeakingGigsNow.com for your FREE GIFT: "The 5 Top Tips to Get Speaking More Gigs Now" You will receive BONUS tips, as well straight out of the vault to help you get your message heard!

About Leisa Reid

Leisa Reid is the Founder of Get Speaking Gigs Now. She mentors entrepreneurs and business professionals who are hoping to attract their ideal clients through speaking.

Chapter 38

---•❖❖•---

Sandrena Schumacher

Devoted Mother & Businesswoman

I was raised in Hong Kong, and I traveled the world with my chef mother. I was drawn to cooking, and I put my own twist on traditional dishes. I'm exceptional at blending international herbs and spices in a way that will delight your palate. I also cater parties ranging anywhere from four to over one hundred people.

I met Eric Zuley through my dear friend Denise Millett Burkhardt. Because of this connection, I now have my own show *Dining with Sandrena*. I cook worldwide cuisine with a twist of fusion. This includes European, Mediterranean, Middle Eastern, Asian, French, and American food. My experience comes from the knowledge I've gleaned by traveling the world and experiencing different cuisine.

Currently, I am involved with a prestigious project for our veterans, in collaboration with Denise Millett Burkhardt, Dr. Dante Sears, and yours truly, Eric Zuley. This will take place in Imperial County, California, where we will treat and heal military veterans. My son Alecsandre Schumacher, will soon be opening an orphanage for widows and orphans of war. I also do fundraising with the LIJUFA International Bowl.

Since Eric has come into my life, I've had so many amazing opportunities to meet like-minded people who want to give back. Attending special events and networking continuously have been very helpful in moving our plans forward.

How to Connect with Sandrena Schumacher:

If you would like me to host your party, or need my assistance with promotional efforts, you may contact me at smapromoting@gmail.com.

Chapter 39

Carmelita Pittman

I met Eric about eight years ago, through the Multicultural Motion Picture Association. I'm very grateful for the moral and professional support I've received from Eric over the years. He and his father have played a large role in my life, and I look forward to working with them for many years to come.

Eric has not only introduced me to some incredible people, but he has given me exposure to a wide variety of audiences. I've been a featured singer at many of his events. I've been featured on the red carpet. I believe in Eric's abilities, and I am constantly astonished by his accomplishments.

About Carmelita Pittman

She was born in Los Angeles. She's been an artist since the age of four, following in her mother's footsteps. She was selected to represent her junior high at Otis Art Institute, and later was asked to represent her high school's theatre arts program. Since then, she has earned the U.S.C. Ross Spayne Perry Award, and has become an award-winning L.A. Unified art educator. Many of her students have gone on to win their own awards and scholarships.

She is also an actress and a dancer. In 1998, she co-sponsored the Pre-Grammy Gala at the Hollywood Roosevelt Hotel.

She founded the Rose Breast Cancer Society as a "living memorial" for her mother, Juanita Zara Espinosa Uddin. The RBCS has received awards from various civic leaders, including Mayor James Hahn and Mayor Antonio Villaraigosa.

She is an accomplished musician as well. She has recorded several Top 40 songs, including "School of Cool," as the rapping teacher Ms. C "Rappin'" Pittman. In 2001, she performed at the Greek Theatre with her students for James Brown. She wrote original songs, including "Rosebud" and "Isn't It Lonely" in collaboration with her husband.

She is an experienced world traveler, and was one of the first Americans to enter remote regions in China along the Marco Polo silk route. Her other travels include treks to Canada, Mexico, Europe, Africa, and Dubai, as well as cross-country excursions in the United States.

She holds a membership with L.A.V.A. (Los Angeles Visual Artists), of which she was a founding member. She is also a member of Sharing Friends of the Arts, Southern California Motion Picture Council, the Multicultural Motion Picture Association, Senior Star Power, RBCC, Artists for a Better World, etc. She attended the Diamond Rose Awards' "Lady in Red" event, where she met Eric Zuley himself.

In 2012, she held the "Ms. American Showbiz" title. She has been dubbed "Ms. Elegance USA" by Woman of Achievement International, a title she held until 2018.

She is the co-founder and art director of the Gardens of Life mural, in collaboration with the Rose Breast Cancer Society. The project has been called an "Alley ART Ography Project." The mural itself has become a cherished treasure in L.A.'s Mid-City community.

Carmelita's keys to success are her strong spiritual beliefs, surrendering her life to the Higher Power, serving humanity, maintaining gratitude, and honoring her mother.

Since 2016, she has co-hosted *Radio Boomers Live!* Her segment is called "Carmelita's Corner." *Radio Boomers Live!* is also co-hosted by Jim Zuley and Reatha Grey. The show can be heard Monday mornings at 10am by calling 1-914-338-1303, or by visiting:

http://www.ezwayradio.com

Find out more at Carmelita's website:
www.rosebreastcancersociety.org

Chapter 40

Aristotle Karas

I've seen Mr. Zuley at numerous industry events, and he always seems to be the person everyone wants to talk to. I didn't really get to know him until the Think and Grow Rich Legacy World Tour, where we shared a stage. I was the auctioneer, and Eric was showing off his dancing skills. That show ended up raising $2500 for a great cause. Since then, I've continued to work with Eric, and I am honored to call him a friend.

About Aristotle Karas

Aristotle is an award-winning auctioneer, speaker, and Amazon best-selling co-author. He has shared stages with Harrison Ford, Morgan Freeman, Les Brown, and Bob Proctor. He has conducted many charity auctions throughout the United States, and is actively involved in the

National Auctioneers Association (NAA). Since 2002, he has helped raise millions of dollars.

He enjoys helping organizations raise money for good causes. He's worked as an auctioneer for events hosted by the Make-A-Wish Foundation, the Special Olympics, the California Women's Convention, Women of Global Change, Saint Jude's Hospital, National Realtors Association, the Humane Society, and the National Honor Society.

He also consults auction teams, working closely with them for up to a year before the event is held. He is widely known for his clear and intelligible speaking voice. Some have even told him he was the first auctioneer they could actually understand.

Aristotle is also a technological trailblazer. He built his own software platform called "The Auction App." He has been featured in several publications, including the NAA's *Auctioneer* and *The Wall Street Journal.*

He holds many esteemed designations from organizations such as the Certified Auctioneer Institute (CAI), and Accredited Auctioneers of Real Estate (AARE). He is one of the few who holds a Benefit Auction Specialist (BAS) designation, a credit fewer than four hundred people in the nation have obtained.

Chapter 41

Heide Hargreaves/D'Angelo

I had a very turbulent upbringing. I won't go into the graphic details, but suffice to say I survived a very rough childhood. I couldn't hear very well. In fact, I was medically deaf. I didn't know how to behave properly, how to make friends, or even use the right words in casual conversation. I spent my youth alienated and alone. I missed out on a lot of the learning and socializing most children get. At home and school, I was  the victim of abuse, bullied by classmates, acquaintances, and family members, just because they perceived me as "different."

Despite my hearing disability, I was able to read lips and body language. I was able to interpret facial expressions. I relied solely on my intuition, and was able to absorb anything visual. For example, I taught myself how to read and write.

Throughout my youth, I longed for a hero to rescue me from the abusive people in my life. I had one teacher who served as a hero of sorts: Mrs. Jean Vemich. She taught me how to listen, speak, and how to do my homework. When so many other people around me either abused me or gave up on me, she stood out. I would not have been able to live a successful life it wasn't for her.

Regardless of the abuse I endured, I still emerged a diamond. I became a determined woman of confidence, capable of taking on any challenge life threw at me. Many people don't understand what it's like living with a disability, but if they did, I think they would be humbler. I believe they would be more compassionate.

When someone has a disability, it does not mean that person is "not abled." It just means that person has to face more challenges than a "normal" person might. I have faced every one of those challenges myself, and each challenge made me a stronger woman. I am not unworthy or substandard. I am not broken.

Despite being legally deaf, I have still spoken on numerous stages, alongside America's top thought leaders, millionaires, and business experts. I have become an author, trainer, instructor, and I'm aspiring to be an influential business leader.

I am a publisher of magazines like *Influential People, International Fitness Fashion, Influential Doctors,* and I host a TV show (also called *Influential People*). I share my experience, wisdom, and success formulas with entrepreneurs from all walks of life, in order to help them transform their businesses. I believe no one should be left out from living a successful life. No one should feel as alone as I felt.

When I met Eric Zuley on social media, he messaged me, asking to be featured in *Influential People.* That message led to an in-person meeting, where we connected and shared our experiences. He interviewed me, and soon became one of my company's contributing partners. Since then, he and I have been working tirelessly to give entrepreneurs and aspiring business leaders more exposure. I am so grateful to have met this incredible young man, and I'm blessed to have the opportunity to collaborate with him.

If you're looking for a family, if you're looking for a supportive group of like-minded friends and colleagues, then look no further than eZWay!

Connect with Heide D'Angelo:
https://www.facebook.com/InfluencerHeideDangelo/
http://www.influentialpeoplemagazine.com
www.fitnessfashionmagazine.com
www.influentialdoctorsmagazine.com
www.influentialpeopleTV.com

Chapter 42

Leila Colgan

I first met Eric at a veteran's event. I was there with a friend who happened to be working with Eric; he needed Eric's help to get his name and presence out into the public's awareness. At this particular event, Eric stood at a podium with his father, and they gave a presentation where they both discussed their faith.

In that moment, I felt an immediate connection with Eric. You don't often hear people proudly discussing their faith in such an open setting. I'm a Christian, and my own faith is very important to me. So when Eric gave that speech, I immediately respected him.

After speaking on faith, Eric changed subjects, and he began talking about building an influence on social media. At that point, I'd been struggling to start my own online business, and when I saw Eric, I immediately knew I could work with this guy. He clearly knew what he was doing, and I knew I could learn a lot from him.

After the presentation, I introduced myself, and as the old expression goes, "the rest is history."

Once we started working together, I introduced Eric to a new social tech platform, similar to Amazon. Eric collaborated with the CEO of that company, and they made plans to do something big with that platform.

Throughout my life, I've always felt as if I was somewhat of a connector. I believe if you can connect with someone on an emotional level, a heart-to-heart level, everything else just falls right into place.

I also consider myself a sales flipper. I can walk into business that's suffering, and I can completely turn it upside-down. I can turn it into a successful business. I've got the technical knowledge, I know what I'm selling, and I actually take the time to get to know my clients. Each one is different, and they all have different needs. I take the time to figure out what those needs are, what I can do for them, and what assistance I can provide. It's not always easy, but I love the challenge!

Working with Eric has taught me to love the challenge. He loves a good challenge, so why shouldn't I? Eric taught me to never let fear steer me away from difficult goals. He believes there is no such thing as failure - there are only experiences that help you learn, grow, and become a better version of yourself.

About Leila Colgan

Leila Colgan is an accomplished healthcare executive, business development leader, entrepreneur and influencer. Her executive leadership experience ranges from small start-up organizations to Fortune 500 companies driving high revenue growth. Leila is a brand influencer for a wellness company where she coaches others how to build an online business, and an Advisor for a new massive social tech platform where she identifies key influencers and enables them to monetize their influence. She is a contributing author in "The Influencer Affect" and is hosting her own TV show "Level up with Leila" with one of the largest networkers in Los Angeles. Leila is an expert connector that helps facilitate relationships that better their business. Leila received her B.A. and Executive MBA from Pepperdine University. She is an active member of several local organizations and a non-profit advocate.

Chapter 43

Tony Boldi

I am Eric's big brother. I met Eric on a red carpet many years ago. He was one of the many people doing them at the time. When he started doing the carpets, it became a big deal. He was right at the beginning of that movement. And then he was right at the beginning of television. Then he was right at the beginning of promoting. Then he was right at the beginning of this and that, and the magazine... It's one of those relationships where we kept  meeting each other at all the events and I was always impressed by his work ethic because he works so hard. I have seen Eric come in as a young kid with a lot of energy and a lot of talent. I would advise him to keep the energy, but to quit giving away all of his expertise. He started to find out how to make money from what he was doing and how to help other people make money. When he started helping others, he really grabbed my interest because he was doing what I had suggested.

I have always respected Eric due to our mutual beliefs. He is a fellow Christian and a serious diehard. He does what he feels is right. I always told him to not worry about the steps to get there, but do it and figure it out as you go. I have been watching him just climb his way forward. I say, fall forward but he never falls forward. He jumps forward. I know of one time that Eric got sick because he worked too hard and ended up in the hospital. I don't know anyone that works as hard as he does. Watching his dad run around with that camera everywhere his son goes, there is something special about that. How can you not love eZ? If I can offer Eric any advice, I do. If he is willing to take it, I will offer.

The fact that he could get to so many A-listers and not pay for them to show up, not even really knowing them was fascinating. Once they got to know him, they were in. Eric introduced me to Larry Namer, founder of entertainment, Frank from Make a Wish and many others. He did those red carpets, built relationships, and followed up. He is the King of Following up! King of Promotion! King of Marketing! King of what to do to become an influencer. This is how you get your numbers. I always thought that Eric should be a billionaire because of the work that he does. He is so close to that next investor, the next sponsor, the one next product endorsement or the other television network. One of these things he has is going to break big. If you want to get to eZ now is the time because if you wait much longer you are not going to afford him at all.

I would like to take a moment and share with you a couple of steps to be successful in the industry.

1. Study your Craft. You have to know what you are diving into and what you are working with. What your instrument can and cannot do.
2. Master craft. Study it, learn it understand it before you showcase it

3. Network. Who are you marketing your craft to. Find your true audience that resonates with what you are doing. Connections are everything so networking and following up are very important.

If you would like to connect with me on a personal level, find me on the Wall of Fame. I want to portray the fact that as we keep exchanging, we ping pong back and forth helping each other to move up. I would love to connect with speakers, authors, upcoming actors and share with them my resources and my experience. The Best You Expo is a special place that I can support all kinds of entrepreneurs in achieving their best self. You can find out more about it at thebestyou.com. I work with actors from the tender age of 4 to 80 years old and promote speakers from all walks of life. I am really looking forward to anchoring the Golden Stage Awards coming very soon. I love doing it the eZWay!

About Tony Boldi

As the Founder and CEO of Lifeforce Foundations, which is a For-Cause Organization focused upon Global and Local Social Concerns, Tony is deeply committed to not only using his talents to amuse and entertain, but as well offer something back to the world. His accolades are almost too numerous to enumerate, but the numerous awards and honors he has received include the Official People's Mayor of Hollywood.

He continues to grow the vast network he has accumulated over the decades as the West Coast Director of Acquisitions for Blairwood Entertainment, as well as becoming the Director of Celebrity Memberships with a top PR/events firm called F.A.M.E. (located in Hollywood, California). Before taking this position, he was the

General Broadcasting Manager of the WCOBM network; while there, he brought in the legendary Pat O'Brien to anchor. He produced, directed, and created two original series at the network: *The Hollywood Review* and *Afternoon Delight*.

Tony started his career as a drummer turned celebrity DJ, getting his big break while working for Mary Jo Slatter in Casting at MGM. As a drummer, Tony has performed with countless celebrities and even won a 2002 Armenian Grammy for best music video of the year; he also won the 1998 New York Film Festival's best new film of the year award.

Additionally, he was the stage director for the 34th Key Art Awards at the famous Academy Awards Kodak Theatre in Hollywood, California. Tony has managed and taught acting to some of the biggest names in Hollywood. He has dealt in everything from financing feature films to directing, writing, producing, editing, and selling his projects from start to finish.

Long before he made his mark in Hollywood, Tony was a candidate for the West Point Academy and received a full ride scholarship to the learning institution of his choice; he chose Western Michigan University, where his mother was the Chairman of the Board of Trustees.

Chapter 44

Brian Willis

I met Eric back in 2014 through Princess Coco Windsor, or we call her Coco. She introduced us at an event. She has been a longtime friend and a member of Billionaire's Elite. The Billionaire's Elite has grown to 5,000 members on our private network, 12,000 on our Facebook Network, and over 2500 professional members on our LinkedIn  Network. Eric is a chairman and our manager, in charge of the group and the network, including the television series. This Elite group is a private professional network. It's global for anyone who wants to feel like a billionaire. I originally made the group to jump on the bandwagon of exclusivity but unfortunately, people took it seriously and thought you had to be a multi-millionaire to be a member. We had a large handful of Royals, and millionaires involved in this network. I never charged a dime for anyone to join, but of course there are requirements to be in the group. Principally it was set up for charitable reasons and for green energy and philosophy. Charities are my passion and some of these include PETA, ASA, and others for human and animal rights.

Eric and I have been long term friends. We always had the same belief system. I am a Christian, Eric is a Christian and we believe in spreading the word of God and being service to others as the Bible teaches. Do unto others as you would have them do unto you. It's always been about being a good human being and believing in a higher power greater than yourself and doing that purpose that is higher than yourself. Eric is running Billionaire's Elite for us and building our Billionaire League Channel that we are executing with him.

Eric's dad, James Zuley is a man after my own heart. I think he has done a great job with Eric and they are my kind of people. I would do anything for these guys and vice versa. We all believe in the same principles of life and carrying on the message and what I out there for others. My expertise is finance and providing financial opportunities for others and major corporations. We are funding over a billion dollars' worth of various programs in different industries through my Singapore company and my Hong Kong Affiliate, and throughout Europe. Eric is the same as I am. I ask myself, am I touching the lives of millions of people daily? I have never seen anyone work as hard as Eric Zuley. As for myself I have slowed down these days. Whenever I go anywhere on Social Media Eric is everywhere. He is a workaholic.

My tips for success are the following:

Never Estimate yourself. You are more powerful than you realize and your potential is that of greatness.

The Results may always be greater than your initial plan so when you plan something be ready for the ride. Create and it will become a creation.

Always treat others as you would like to be treated.

Dare to be all you can be. That's it. Just dare and jump.

I am the guy behind the scenes and I keep a low profile, but when something important is put before me I am there for all. I know a lot of people with power but I am myself and that is what I want people to see. That I am me. Brian Willis. I love humanity.

I am proud to affiliate with Eric Zuley. It is always easier to do it the eZWay.

About Brian Willis

Brian N. Willis is an international financier, humanitarian, and philanthropist. He is a founding member of Billionaire's Elive VIP, with over 20,000 members globally. The Billionaires Elive VIP Club was created for very special and professional individuals for networking purposes.

Mr. Willis is also active with the Republican Congressional Committee and is an honorary co-chairman to the Republican Business Advisory Board for the State of California. He is well respected for his ambition, vast ranging knowledge, and exemplary leadership, and has received a number of awards as the Republican Presidential Honor Role under President Donald J. Trump, Top 100 Registry of Business Leaders, Marquis Who's Who in America 2017-2018, including Business Man of the Year for 2005 and 2006, Republican of the Year for 2006, a Congressional Medial of Distinction, a Congressional Order of Merit, Who's Who inclusions for years 1995, 1996, and 2002, a Certificate of Recognition from the International Commission, and an honorary Doctor of Philosophy from the International Royal Academy of the United Nations. Mr. Willis complements this remarkable profile with an equally commendable array of philanthropic pursuits. He works with various humanitarian groups and charities including the Christian Children's Fund and the Foundation for Our Children's Children (FFOCC). Mr. Willis is also a frequent contributor to such causes as the Red Cross and Feed the Children.

Chapter 45

Josh Liske

I met Eric Zuley at Speaking Empire. He was speaking on stage about sponsorship and how to make money at your event with sponsors. When he was done speaking I spoke to one of his team members about joining the membership. A couple of months later I was on Magazine Covers, stages, with a book coming out and all kinds of suc-cess. Eric presented me with the "Mentor of the Year" award for the eZWay Wall of Fame Awards where I was able to network and meet some amazing people. He opened doors for me to get on new stages and it has been an amazing experience.

My tips for success include the following:

Relationship equity – It isn't what you know, it isn't even who you know, rather who knows you. Get yourself seen and heard. Make the connections and let yourself shine. Give people the opportunity to know you by attending events, getting on stages, and introducing yourself.

Power of Association – You are who you associate with. Partner with people whom you look up to and want to be like. Find others who share your same faith and morals and belief systems and serve them. Get involved with the groups of people that will raise you up to their standards and uphold yours.

Last but not least, Put God first ALWAYS. Putting your higher power to the forefront and highest of priorities will guarantee the success you can't even imagine. He wants you to succeed and you are divinely created to magnify your calling in this life. He will raise you up. Just have faith.

Do it the eZWay. It has worked for so many and has worked for me.

About Josh Liske

At the age of 18 he started going door to door for two years and within 18 months became a leader and a recruiter for six of those months. Just a few years later he became a branch manager and a direct distributor CEO. In July of 2018 he took over the Division in Australia as a divisional leader and now he oversees 50 offices and about 500 people in the Midwest. His 22 years of experience have brought him to his great success today where his office was the number one ranking in 2014 out of fifteen hundred other offices and over fifty-five plus nations. Nicknamed "Elevator", he raised 19 CEO's to the highest level in his industry. Out of a burning desire to help CEO's grow their offices and senior pastors grow their congregations, he has cast a vision and focus on the future with a big vision of global healing. His talent as a life and leadership coach and authorship have given him the opportunity to motive and lift others to their success.

In 2016 he founded and built IHP Global with his wife Gina Liske. They both know that where they are headed is probably more important than what they have accomplished. The burning desire that they are creating has created a vision of bringing families together and building strong relationships on unity and forgiveness. His unconditional love for others is his heart, and his passion is to have a children's camp in Costa Rica of Restoration.

Currently attending Destiny College, of Florida, he will have a doctorate in Leadership in the next 18 months. Building others to "Elevate" themselves to a higher standard is what he loves the most and it is prevalent in all that he does.

Already an author and award winning Business Man, his newest and upcoming book "Elevate" will bring masterminds and experts to the table with advice and inspiration to create more leaders in our world. He aspires to lift others to the highest levels of success. Josh Liske is definitely on our watch list as this "Mentor of The Year" sprints forward in action to create a bigger impact and influence on the world at large.

Braintapping is a quick and easy way to relax, reboot and revitalize by simply optimizing your brain's peak potential—anytime, anywhere. Backed by neuroscience and research, braintapping is proven to help people who experience high stress, difficulty sleeping, low energy, and other lifestyle challenges.

NON-BRAINTAPPING	BRAINTAPPING
Prone to stress	Stress-free
Experience anxiety	Calm and controlled
Difficulty controlling weight	Able to control weight
Low energy or mood	Energetic and positive
Brain fog	Clarity of thought
Poor health	Healthy

Braintapping guides your mind from an awake, reactionary mind into an intuitive, creative state, then to a place where super-learning and healing can occur, with the outcome being a heightened state of consciousness with crystal clear focus. Unlike meditation programs, BrainTap's exclusive neuro-algorithms gently and naturally guide your brain through a broad range of brainwave patterns, instead of just the Alpha state. The result is a complete spectrum of brainwave activity.

Use this One time QR Code to get your gift from BrainTap for purchasing this book. Lock in savings on a product that will truly change your life. This offer is only good to redeem one per household.

Thank you BrainTap for supporting The Influence Effect and doing it the eZWay!

Get Access For A Year & Save

~~$239~~ $199/year

GET OFFER

Lock In Your Savings!
Bundle with a headset and keep your low subscription price forever.

SUBSCRIPTION + BRAINTAP HEADSET
The Most Impactful, Immersive Experience

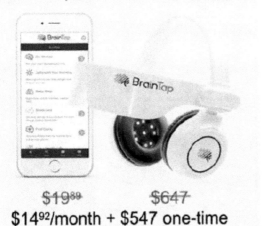

~~$19⁸⁹~~   ~~$647~~
$14⁹²/month + $547 one-time

 CPSIA information can be obtained
at www.ICGtesting.com
Printed in the USA
LVHW050905161120
671800LV00003B/403